About the Author

Having made a career lecturing on problem solving and leadership in a business school, John decided it was time to walk the talk and put the theory into practice. He thought he would find the physical side hardest but it was his poor decision making and struggle to cope with loneliness that surprised him.

John Rayment

COAST LINES

AUSTIN MACAULEY™
PUBLISHERS LTD.

A CIP catalogue record for this title is available from the British Library.

ISBN 9781786298539 (Paperback)
ISBN 9781786298546 (Hardback)
ISBN 9781786298553 (E-Book)

www.austinmacauley.com

First Published (2017)
Austin Macauley Publishers Ltd.™
25 Canada Square
Canary Wharf
London
E14 5LQ

Coast Lines

Coast Lines

Pictures of places seen on a walk

Photos of faces – my how they talk

The tale of a stroll round the coast of GB

Tilbury to Tilbury – and back home for tea.

Talk the Walk

Is this the first of three such books?
It will be if I make it
Each part of a longer tale
That is, if you can take it
Come on a trip round GB's coast
In verse and photos told
I think you'll find it mind-blowing
If I may be so bold
You'll find you cannot put it down
Can't swap it for another
Not because the tale's so strong
But I've super-glued the cover

Dedication

Before I end, 'fore I begin
There's a secret I'll let you in
I'd never have made it
Without my Lynn

August 2012:
Best Foot Forward

Seeking to raise 'a penny a pace'
While walking round GB
Donating it to Parkinson's
A cause that's dear to me

Wore this logo on my shirt
So everyone could see
I put my best foot forward
Please buy a book or three

Planning

August First of Twenty Twelve I headed out the door
The way I guess I must have done ten thousand times or more
But never such a sketchy plan nor major task before
"Find the sea; turn right (or left?!) then walk the GB shore"

Being faced with such a task you'd need a basic plan
Carry everything you need? A rucksack? Campervan?
Accommodation in advance or casual as you went?
Spend the nights in B&B's or sleeping bag in tent?
How far is it round GB's coast? 6,000 miles – or more?
How many miles, day after day weary and foot-sore?

Getting Going

I'd always fancied walking round my homeland's rugged coast
So on the 1st of August when I'd finished all my toast
Threw some bits and pieces into my rucksack bag
Change of clothing, waterproofs, trousers and a cag
'Don't want too much to carry on my back or in my mind'
So bundled up my worries and left them all behind

'So where should I start walking?' as I slowly closed the door
'Need to cross the river Thames but where the closest shore?
Guess it must be Tilbury, there's a ferry by the dock
Use that to cross to Gravesend then keep going as the clock
Pick up the coastal footpath and follow it through Kent'
So with good thoughts and wishes picked up my bag and went

Seeking A Cure

I'd be walking to raise money and awareness of PD
Graham Green read a poem as we gathered at Tilbury
Written 12 years earlier 'bout my father mum and us
Coping with the hurt and pain "Mustn't make a fuss"
Expressing our frustrations that no-one had found a cure
Was then I'd started thinking of a GB coastal tour
Taking on the challenges: body brain and soul
Would I have the fitness – or be driven round the pole?

So there I stood as fear and dread made me doubt my choice
"That is something I don't have" said my PD conscience voice.

There Must Be A Way

Silently fighting day after day

Trapped inside watching your building decay

Forced to a mumble defiant you say

"If there is a God... There must be a way"

Silently helping day after day

Trapped beside watching you lover decay

True dedication cheerful you stay

Screaming inside: "God, there must be a way"

Silently sharing day after day

Trapped outside watching your lives ebb away

How can we help you? Frustrated we pray:

"Logic or magic, God show us the way"

Hitting the ~~Bottle~~ Road

A fab send off at Tilbury
But how some folk did squawk
When I leapt up on the ferry
"A strange way to start a *walk*!"

Friends came across to Gravesend
For a coffee and a chat
But I had to get my rucksack on
And "Farewell to all that"
Eloise said she'd do a mile
To get me on my feet
Then Gabby walked another six
To be sure I didn't cheat

Industry meadows and farmland led along the shore
'That's day 1 done and dusted –
Just three hundred and ninety-nine more'

Bye Bye Blues

First two days were pleasant strolls
Day three brought a frown
Niggly little things went wrong
I let them get me down
All is fine yet I feel low
Anti-climax from the start?
Made up a rather morbid poem
To fit my heavy heart

Leaden Heart

Do you know what it's like
To watch your lover go?

Have you seen as they slowly fade
From what they've been?

Leaden heart as you feel
Their energy depart

Bye Bye Bye Bye Blues

Must have been thinking about the task, PD and my dad
Leaving friends and family would make anyone feel sad
But having got it off my chest my spirits rose again
Except that I was rushing when I wanted to refrain

Only made eleven miles before an early stop
To attend a farewell party and a final line dance bop
I'll feel fine tomorrow – 1% complete, thank God
I know what you are thinking: Cheer up you miserable sod!

Day 4 was great, so very pleased I made it past day 3
Joined for the sunny afternoon by colleague Natalie
Saw a seal just bobbing along, covered 18 miles
Raised £210 the previous night, all helped replace my smile

Stubble Trouble

This field looked an easy path, just scoot along the rows
Without a worry in the world, forgetting all my woes
How would a townie lad like me foresee the hidden trouble
In all that tough and razor-sharp boot-lacerating stubble?

Getting It Off My Chest

One thing was still preventing me relax, enjoy, unwind
I felt my ex-employer hadn't treated me too kind
Needed to sort my feelings so I put them into verse
Should help me feel much better, hopefully not worse
Then we both can chill and focus on the task in hand
Stroll along the winding coast of this green and pleasant land

Facing The Axe

If you've worked for one employer
The last 30 years and more
When a confidential letter
Comes a'crashing through your door
Take care it's just the letter
That falls crumpled to the floor

"We've got all kinds of assets
But our staff are number one
So 'though you've worked here most your life
Your days with us are done
Your teaching skills are first rate but
No PhD old son"

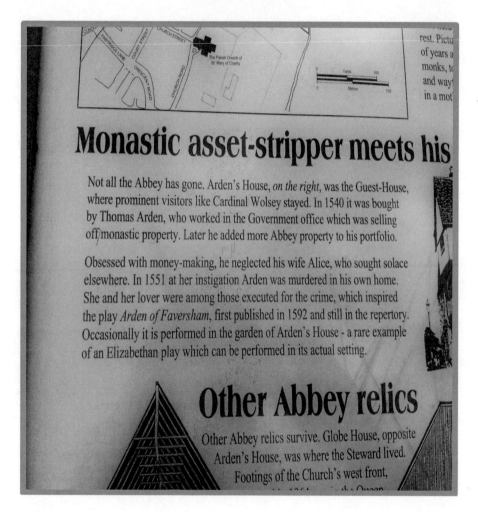

Monastic asset-stripper meets his

Not all the Abbey has gone. Arden's House, *on the right*, was the Guest-House, where prominent visitors like Cardinal Wolsey stayed. In 1540 it was bought by Thomas Arden, who worked in the Government office which was selling off/monastic property. Later he added more Abbey property to his portfolio.

Obsessed with money-making, he neglected his wife Alice, who sought solace elsewhere. In 1551 at her instigation Arden was murdered in his own home. She and her lover were among those executed for the crime, which inspired the play *Arden of Faversham*, first published in 1592 and still in the repertory. Occasionally it is performed in the garden of Arden's House - a rare example of an Elizabethan play which can be performed in its actual setting.

Other Abbey relics

Other Abbey relics survive. Globe House, opposite Arden's House, was where the Steward lived. Footings of the Church's west front,

"True you've done all that we asked
You're highly skilled and able
But 'Percent of staff with PhDs'
Will lift us up the table
And though your research is first rate
You haven't got that label"

"We're a modern university so
Teaching's not our role
It's 'climbing the league table'
That's now our only goal
But we'll give you several grand to go
To prove we have a soul"

It took a few days thinking
Just to get me through the shock
Being told you're just not wanted
Could be a vicious knock
But what an opportunity
To take my life in stock

Yes, opportunities like this
Come rarely it would seem
For now I had money and time
To live my lifelong dream
To walk the coast of Britain
Over clifftop beach and stream

Positive Thoughts

It worked again
Thoughts made plain
Took away the pain
Their loss: my brain
Freedom: my gain

Holistic Fitness

Severance gave the chance
To test my holistic fitness
Physical, mental, spiritual
Myself the only witness
Achieve a long-term dream
And raise money for PD
Be madness to refuse it
The rest was up to me

Relaxing Into The Walk

Eight days, a quarter million steps and feeling great!!
Towns, ports, castles – Rochester, Reculver and Margate
Interesting coastline, beaches, Sandwich's golf courses
Seagulls, seals, sheep and goats, cows, ponies and horses
Two percent – at this rate I'll be back at Tilbury
31st October '13 in time for afternoon tea

A final verse for 'Facing The Axe' came readily to mind
As Dover shone through lifting mist, my doubt now far behind

'We've decided to give you Severance
So clear your desk and head
You'll never need to work again
Can spend your days in bed'
I thought they'd chop my hand off
But they gave me cash instead!

A Sharp Reminder

Don't be disturbed by this photo
But if you must enquire
Slipped on steps, grabbed the fence
Got skewered on barbed wire

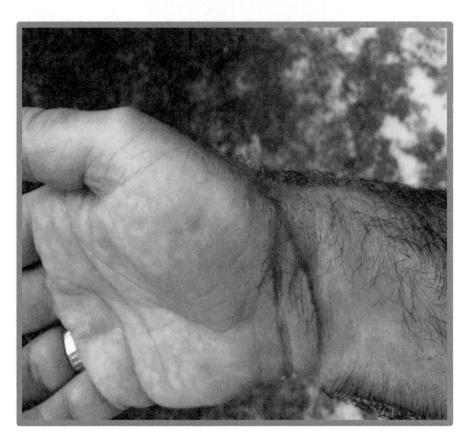

It was a sharp reminder of
The paths oft' hidden dangers
Must take care walking alone
Not take ice creams from strangers

Early days build fitness for
The tougher ones ahead
Remote, tough, tricky places where
I'd need to watch my tread

Had to keep my efforts
Within my scope and power
Didn't want to end up crooked
Like this Pisaoidal tower

Up To My Neck

Joined by friends at Eastbourne, up and over Beachy Head
"The sea looks so inviting" their seductive daughter said
So suddenly I'm swimming and thinking with a grin
"I've walked beside it day on day, guess it's time that I got in"

Para Olympic Plod

Starting August 2012 meant Olympics London clash
I could have started after and some folks thought me rash
Wasting a perfect summer watching others just seemed lazy
With a mega challenge of my own, I thought it would be crazy
There'd always be a reason for putting off the start
Inside I knew the time was right so followed head and heart

Image by Thomas from Northease Manor School

Cleft Cliff

All along this stretch of coast
The cliffs stand proud and white
Adding to the UK's claim
Of independent might
But making it so difficult
For locals to go fishing
"Unless somebody cut a road"
You can almost hear them wishing

Save Me! Save Me!

I've got to be responsible
And take my own precautions
Lady Luck shares her favours
In realistic portions

But if it comes to self-recue
I may not try too hard
Just call 'Save me! Save me!'
And wait for the lifeguard

Day	Start	End
1	Tilbury	Upnor
2	Upnor	Upchurch
3	Upchurch	Sittingbourne
4	Sittingbourne	Faversham
5	Faversham	Herne bay
6	Herne bay	Broadstairs
7	Broadstairs	Deal
8	Deal	Folkestone
9	Folkestone	Dungeness
10	Dungeness	Rye
11	Rye	Hastings
12	Hastings	Eastbourne
13	Eastbourne	Seaford
14	Seaford	Brighton

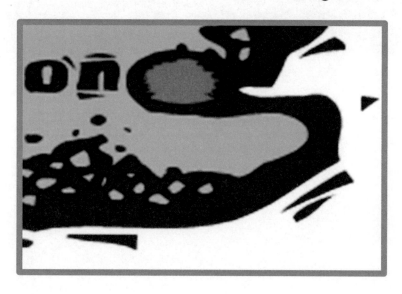

Always Plenty More

From Brighton through to Pagham
Miles of broad flat sandy beach
Soft and dry then flat and wet
The sea far out of reach

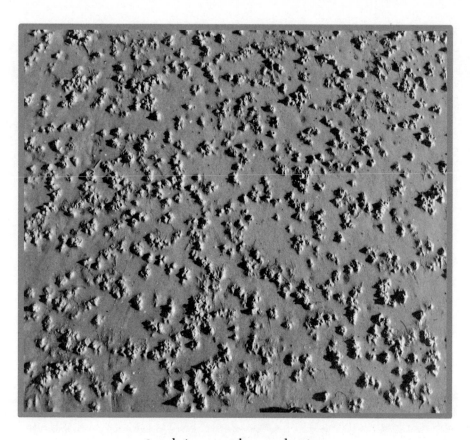

Sandpiper, curlew and snipe
Feed along the shore
But worm casts by the million show
There's always plenty more

Street Art

Modern buildings, street furniture and statues look so cool
Fantastic fabrics, shapes and styles breaking every rule
Littlehampton had some which I found extremely neat
This being a café, the next benches and seat

Pay Attention

Given my poor track record (see 'Mister Blister' novel)
I knew I must be well prepared or end up in some hovel
Still hadn't given close enough attention to the tide

An hour ago an easy step, but now too deep and wide
Added another three miles when I really didn't need it
Another path lesson well learnt – that is, if I should heed it

i For Idiot

Using my phone for web access, texts, calls, camera and maps
Saved me lots of space and weight but came with subtle traps
If it was lost or stolen, broken, anything like that
Or given all the constant use the battery goes flat?
Maps were on ViewRanger I could zoom in and out
Showed my exact location and direction with no doubt
But I was having problems and my heart began to sink

Phone suddenly stopped working – the charger on the blink

Keeping Count and Calorie Control

One thing I wasn't using my phone for was counting paces
Done by the gadget shown below, attached to belt or braces

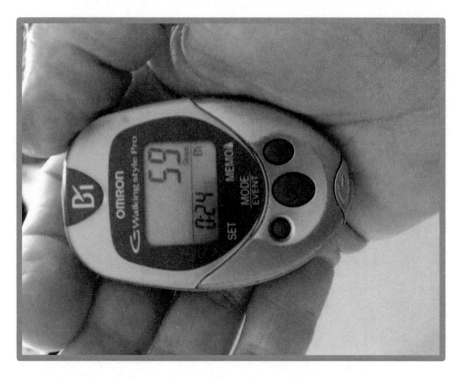

I'd entered 80cms as my assumed average gait
100kgs including pack as my total weight
Output: day and total steps and calories I'd burnt
At 125 a mile, 16 miles 2,000 earnt

To maintain weight I needed 4,500 ev'ry day
But could do with losing some, 12-14 pounds let's say
Maybe lose two stones of fat and gain a stone of muscle
Surely a fair and just reward for all my toil and bustle

What's Mine Is Jaws

I saw this guy tie up his boat after a great day's fishing
Found myself, I couldn't help, wondering and wishing
Would I swap my life for his if I could make selection
Didn't take me long though to reject for, on reflection
I could see his lacked something, was it possibly a mate?
I pondered did he have one who had met a dreadful fate
I think I'll just stick with my walk if it's all the same
In case, a kind of double bluff, the answer's in the name

Island Hopping

Day 19 I found out about the Hayling Island ferry
Faster route to Portsmouth so was sure to make me merry
Though it meant another long day over 20 mile
I'd earn some short and easy, a thought to make me smile

Backpackers hostel and fitful sleep 'though in a cosy bed
My room-mates' varied noises ring and echo round my head
Restless rustling papers, drinking, going to the loo
Woken at 7.00 by their alarm: I nearly threw my shoe

But soon I saw the funny side and took it like a man
Lucky, 'cos they were on leave from tour: Afghanistan
And while they were our soldiers so couldn't be all bad
Dread to think where my iPhone may have ended if I had

Time to head for the Isle of Wight via hovercraft
Find my work pal Graham and join him for a draught
Meet my daughter and family take the weekend off
My first break since Tilbury in beautiful Bournemouth

Green and Wet

Enjoying the sun on an easy day allowed my mind to wander
Bang! At the bottom of this ramp I had something to ponder

Rubbing my elbow and backside, face pained with regret
I hadn't learnt to never walk on a surface green and wet
To get over my aches and pains, not wallow in self pity
I took my usual exit route of making up a ditty

When I see weed I see seaweed
It makes me shake with fear
I scream and scream
I scream... ice-cream
Now that's a good idea!

Unhelpful Signs

Signs like this just made me hoot
Why closed? What dates?
Alternate route?
Would a fit walker be safe to go?
Or serious danger and 'No Means No'?

This time I found a lovely lane

But poor signs really are a pain

The morning after the night before

The morning after the night before
(Several beers and a curry)
Then Graham came to Keyhaven
Where we lunched in a hurry

We had no time for afters
So Marian and I instead
Bought ourselves an ice cream that
Lasted to Hengistbury Head

Walker's Holiday

I had a rest day scheduled
Planned to take it at my ease
Playing with my grandchildren
Cameron and Eloise

Persuaded them to join me
For 8-miles to Sand Banks
To be early on the SWCP
Well done kids and thanks

Know what you're thinking, reader
Rather dirty tricks
But I was getting desperate
Yes really in a fix

Planned Euro-Disney trip with them
Was making me pull my hair
My train left Plymouth the day before
My walk plan got me there

So even with this fiddle
If anything went wrong
I'd arrive in Plymouth
When my Euro-train had gone

The SWCP Challenge

How far could I go I wanted to know
Were my legs sufficiently stout?
How well would I plan? Need a tent or a van
To keep the weather out?
Would a pain or a strain get to my brain
And leave me full of doubt?

Would I mould to the walk or to myself talk
As I wound around the shore?
Take time to chill or make myself ill
Exhausting myself to the core?
Enjoy the space away from the race
Or find it and myself a bore?

Would I find my soul or go round the pole
As the miles went slowly by?
Would I meet my God as I trod His sod
And gaze into His eye
Would He lighten my load or on some dark road
Would my Devil come riding by?

Missing Link

You'd be forgiven for thinking this
The Needles, Isle of Wight
But in fact it is Old Harry Rocks
An equally lovely sight
The two once joined by solid cliff
Now 15 miles apart
'Cross Christchurch, Poole and Studland bays
It's shown here on my chart

Facing The Light

Tim Cumming is an artist
Raising money for PD
His paintings celebrate progress
That's very plain to see
Being made by researchers
Seeking a final cure
When he said "Can I paint you?"
My immediate answer "Sure"

Getting Even

I walked the Isle of Portland, not mainland coast I know
But on the South West Coast Path so felt I ought to go
Walked it anti-clockwise to gain different points of view
Even any muscle strain and straighten up my shoe

Summer crops were ripening in golden swaying rows
Cut, rolled, baled, collected, see how the haystack grows

Treat Your Feet

Chisel Beach looked fab but
All those pebbles on these feet?!
SWCP Guide's suggestion:
Go inland of The Fleet

Till then I'd worn old running shoes
They'd given me no trouble
But holes were appearing and the air
Had gone out their bubble

It had been raining plenty
Better take care of my feet
Put on my big boy's walking boots
To give them a little treat

I expected my feet to carry me
Regardless of the weather
Least I could do in gratitude
Was cover them in leather

Time

Walking along the Jurassic Coast
I hoped to find a fossil
But didn't dig my strict schedule
Made that quite impossil
Six thousand miles in reasonable time
Must compromise it seems
Couldn't enjoy the places I passed
- An important part of my dreams

I had no time for a decent dig
No time to 'stand and stare'
May come back for a proper look
When I have time to spare

Near the end of my first walk month
So time for some reflection
How did I feel I'd done so far

Was it in the right direction?!
I thought my progress fantastic
Was really enjoying the walk
Not lonely as I'd feared I'd be
Although I missed the talk

But I had no time for a decent dig
No time to 'stand and stare'
Will come back for a proper look
When I have time to spare

Pleased to have found my target pace
Fifteen miles a day all right
But this the easy time of year
Warm days, plenty of light
Shops, cafes, B+Bs open
And on the easy ground
I expected tougher times ahead
Mustn't let that get me down

Though I'd have no time for a decent dig
No time to 'stand and stare'
Must come back for a proper look
When I have time to spare

Twelve more months walking alone
Remote, tough, lonely places
Constant pressure of the clock
Putting me through my paces
Whether I could gear up then
There really was no knowing
Tell myself 'When the going gets tough
Is when the tough get going'

When it's over I'll have time for a decent dig
When it's over I'll 'stand and stare'
Then I'll come back for a proper look
Then I'll have time to spare

Number Slumber

Quite aware my maths didn't work
I'd chosen to ignore it
Now I felt the time was right
To cautiously explore it
My plan was 6,000 miles at
15 mpd
Dividing comes to 400 days
As anyone can see

To finish end October '13
I had just 457
If I could somehow make that work
I'd surely be in heaven
But it only gave 57 days off
Less than one a week
While a decent 3-month winter break
Was something else I'd seek

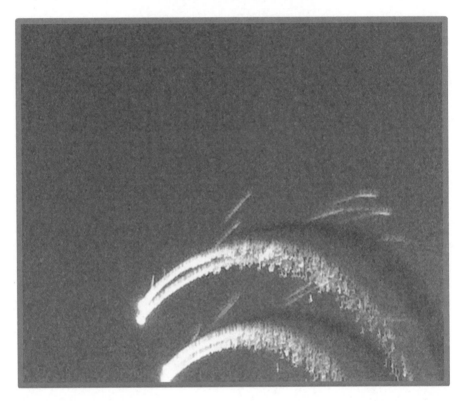

Part to enjoy Christmas and New Year
With family around
But no point winter walking
With no people to be found
For me to raise more money from
Chat to about PD
Unconcerned about bad weather
Yes, rather naively

I knew short daylight hours
Might put my mileage out
Or lead me into danger
With few rescuers about
My solution? Wait and see!
Dear reader, please don't scoff
You know I never make a choice
If I can put it off!

Last Day of Month 1

Walk Day 28 started on
Weymouth's fantastic sand
Raked soft and smooth an ideal base
For holidaymakerland
The Weymouth Harbour ferryman
Still used a rowing boat
Wouldn't take my money, said
"Stick it in your float"

It was perfect walking weather
Still I wondered as I went
"Am I losing too much weight
Or did I just see an Ent?"

Set my sights on Abbotsbury
Far end of The Fleet
Where thousands of swans gather
Chisel Beach to meet

Halfway to Abbotsbury heard
This secret from a horse
"Other grass is greener" hence
The long face, of course

Finding the walk fantastic
But it still felt rather weird
When on the stroke of midnight
My work email disappeared
32 years gone in a flash
But taking off the mask
Freeing me to concentrate
On my current task

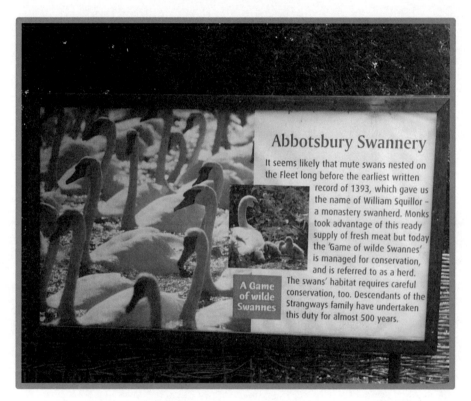

My Swan Song

Day	Start	End
15	Brighton	Worthing
16	Worthing	Bognor
17	Bognor	West Wittering
18	West Wittering	Bosham
19	Bosham	Portsmouth
20	Portsmouth	Cowes
21	Cowes	Lymington
22	Lymington	Hengistbury Head
23	Hengistbury Head	Sandbanks
24	Sandbanks	Worth Maltravers
25	Worth Maltravers	Lulworth Cove
26	Lulworth Cove	Weymouth
27	Isle of Portland	Isle of Portland
28	Weymouth	Swyre

September 2012
The Angel of Noss Mayo

Keeping Grounded

Start of month two and I felt great
Fit and strong and losing weight
Got to keep my thinking sound
Feet and feelings on the ground
One month done and well on track
But mustn't think 'I'm nearly back'
Though confidence was high and growing
Persuaded myself I was 'just getting going'

What's in a Name?

You find some strange stuff on the path
Oftentimes it makes you laugh
I've heard folks call a spade a spade
But when I saw this, I'm afraid
Another term sprang to the fore
A shit shovel, no less no more

A Deadly Warning

Summer was extremely wet
And now a sign lest we forget
Another walker here had died
Victim of a huge mudslide
Coast guards had to close the breach
I risked the walk along the beach
Offering a silent prayer
For Charlotte Blackman buried there

Appreciate the Maintenance Task

The more I walked the more I saw
The fragile nature of our shore
How difficult the coastguards' role:
Keep me safe throughout my stroll
Aiming to maintain the truce
'Tween owner, walker, other use
Balancing demand and budget -
Increasingly I knew I'd fudge it

Kept this in mind as I left Charmouth
On a landslide detour to soaking Sidmouth
Seventeen miles became twenty-two
Met my next host Rupert Bannister who
Kept me entertained for hours and hours
Feared neither distance nor incessant showers
But even for frogs who don't mind the rain
The sun on your back is a positive gain

Time to Celebrate?

My one millionth step somewhere here
This sign also cheered me it's clear
But Rupert said "NO,
We've too far to go
There's no time for a Beer beer I fear

Rupert then put me up for the night
Next day ensured I started right
Drove me in his van
To my start point. Good man
But still owes me a Beer beer on sight

Let the Train Take the Strain

While this journey's fantastic by train
Steep soft cliffs make erosion a pain
And this stretch of the line
Swung in air, undermined
By the next winter's heavy rain

Something's A Foot

John Gammans joined me for a couple of days
Let's give him and Vicky the requisite praise
Provided my transport, meals and a bed
"I'll carry your gear in my bag" John then said

Suddenly weightless, shoulders reached for the sky
Bouncing along but my throat felt quite dry
Twitchy, uneasy as if there was a catch
My bag was my pal – we'd grown attached
Then disaster struck – A BLISTER! O M G!!
But I'm spiritually fit so it couldn't stop me

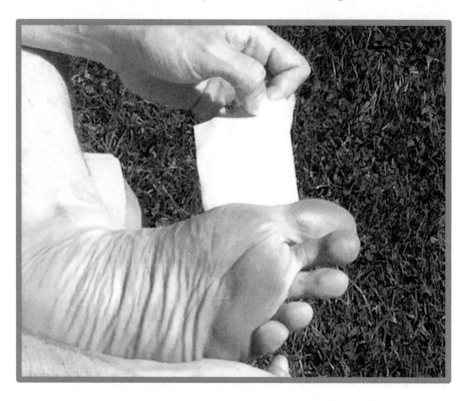

OK I confess the last line isn't quite true
It was on JG's foot and not mine – selfish phew!

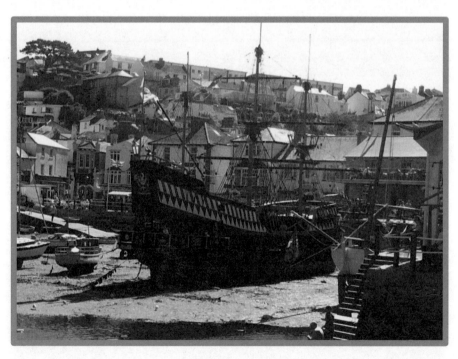

Wake Up and Pay Attention

Had one day alone then joined by Steve P
Who walked for two days to famous Bigbury
I very nearly trod on an adder – mistake!
Steve claimed it to be a tiny grass snake
But he who laughs last laughs longest you know
And I have the evidence – just check below

Double Crossed

At Bigbury spied a noticeboard which
Held info I'd need to cross river or ditch
Including the Erme – I'd soon cross that river
Missed that for the Yealm – which still makes me shiver

But crossing the Erme would be no easy ride
Could only be done if close to low tide
Which the tide table showed as 4.30am
Or late afternoon at 17.10

What to do?

Walk three to five-thirty, arrive with the lark –
And risk walking cliff paths alone in the dark?

Follow the river to the first bridge's span –
Add seven extra miles to the 20 now planned?

Or wait 'til the arvo, at least 16.10 -
With 15 more miles to my B&B then?

Hardly my dream walk with never a care
And as you know I don't like tearing my hair

I thought for some time but the choice wasn't clear
Steve said "Sure we can solve it... over a beer"

But when my eyes fell on this fine figurehead

Decided I'd ask her for guidance instead

Beseeched her to act as my guide, friend and coach
Steve chose a less subtle, more direct approach
I guess he just felt uncontrollable lust
Took two paces forward and assaulted the bust

I asked a lifeguard for advice and she said
"There's a rusty old bridge that you could try instead
A little up river – I think it's still there
Crumbling and rotten – so use it with care"
There was something I felt in the tone of her voice
That deepened the warning, but was it a choice?

My eventual solution: to start around eight
Walk to the Erme and... leave it to fate
Not much of a plan but what else could I do?

Of course at the time I still hadn't a clue
That a far worse disaster was waiting in store
The Yealm with its ferry that closed sharp at four

Once one thing goes wrong I find troubles soon grow
And now I discovered another slight woe
I had a room booked in the Royal Oak pub
Famous for fine beers and quality grub
But two miles inland up a steep winding track
Another straw placed on this poor camel's back

Cumulative Stupidity

Next day ended one of the best
Yet half an hour into my quest
It near drove me mad
When I found I still had
The pub room keys close to my chest

Could have sent them back in the post
But decided I needed a roast
So returned to the inn
Then set out again
Done four miles 'fore I reached the coast

Five miles to the Erme, reached at twelve
My lift dream I soon had to shelve
And no-one around
I might well have drowned
If I'd taking the swim on myself

I had nine miles under my belt
But imagine the anguish I felt
When I read on the sign
It was 'Noss Mayo 9'
A tough hand – and to myself dealt

Forced to search for another way out
A sign writer confirmed all my doubt
If too far by tracks he
Suggested "a taxi"!
This day's turning into a rout

Seven more, twenty-five that would be
Which I knew was about max for me
But was just to Noss Mayo
I'd still be on my way ("oh –
Still don't know of the Yealm river ferry")

Perhaps I *Should* Swim Across?!

Before he'd approve my coast walk
My son made me solemnly swear
I would do nothing stupid (!) like swim
Rivers 'alone and out there'

This proved very helpful to me
As facing rough times on the track
I didn't have the 'go on, you wimp'
Dare Devil there on my back

Thought 'No, promised Peter' instead
And wimped out without any qualms
Helped me maintain my self-respect
No drowning, broken legs or arms

Didn't help with the extra miles, though

A Decision!

I decided to seek the rotten old bridge
That's if it still existed
A vehicle track marked on my map
Locked gates with barb-wire twisted

Walking the lane but seeking a break
Found a hole in the hedge
Wonderful path through late summer woods
Led right to the river edge

I struggled through nettles, brambles and briars
And pools of oozing mud
Risking a bath when leaping wide streams to
Finally reach the flood

At last I found the rotten old bridge
Full of holes and rust
Heart in my mouth 'What would Peter say?
But get across I must'

Another good path back to the crossing
Now on the other side
It was 2.00pm so two hours lost
Still I felt a glow of pride

Until I read the warning sign
Yealm?! Ferry?! Stops at four!

1	1812
1	1948
4	2111
1	2208
31	2255
16	2337
57	– –
18	1238
58	1318
138	1358
217	1438
259	1522
344	1613
0439	1717
0551	1842
0720	2010
0840	2118
0940	2210
1029	2255
1113	2335
1152	– –

ontact the
onb.org.uk

River Dart

A passenger and vehicle ferry runs a continuous service, 7am - 10.55pm daily throughout the year.

River Yealm

A ferry service operates across the Yealm from 1st April until 30th September 2012. It runs everyday from 10am – 4pm, although in bad weather and quieter times the service is restricted to 10am – 12noon and 3pm – 4pm. The ferryman, Bill Gregor, can be contacted on 07817 132757.

Salcombe Estuary

A passenger ferry runs daily all year, 8am - 5.30pm in winter. 8.30am - 5.30pm at weekends and bank holidays. 8am - 6.30pm in summer, possibly up to 7pm in August. The ferryman, Simon Shortman, can be contacted on 01548 842061.

Cursed and raged my stupidity
How had I missed it before?!

I'd felt pretty smug, now a bungling fool
How had I been so blind?
Two hours left for another nine miles
I was really in a bind

Many a steep up and down, heavy pack
Over rough terrain
No real choice but to go for it and...
Trust to luck – again

Took a photo of the phone number
Hoping though I was late
I'd get to chat to the ferryman and
Persuade him to wait

You Only Cheat Yourself

I could have made it easily
Taking an inland route
Roads straight and flat
But what point in that?
Gave that idea the boot

Would mean I hadn't done the path
Of course no-one would know
Except for me
But I'm sure you see
I'd challenged myself to go

So I stuck to the route as my ferry chance
Became increasingly fleeting
I strode along
Singing this song
'It's only yourself you'd be cheating'

Ups and Downs

Two men jogged by
Made me all but cry
Then brought me to my senses
I'd done umpteen miles
O'er rivers and styles
O'er hills and dales and fences

With pack on back
Still yet to crack
And many miles ahead
'I'll catch that boat
My turn to gloat
While stretching in my bed'

The last five miles
Was full of smiles
On a Victorian carriage drive
'To Noss Mayo
My feet must go
But I feel so alive'

I finally rang
The ferryman
'Are you sitting in it?

I've done twenty mile'
I felt his cruel smile
"That's great – you've got 5 minutes"

The Angel of Noss Mayo

Just after five
When I arrived
The jetty was deserted
Muttered 'Oh well'
And 'What the hell'
But slightly disconcerted

'I'll find the pub
Get me some grub
And then somewhere to sleep
Be the first night
I've not got it right'
But my problems had been a heap

Then through the trees
Saw a shop selling teas
With three ladies chatting outside
'Can I get across?'
But with a head toss
"Not until early morning" one sighed

I spoke of my quest
And need for a rest
B&B booked on t'other side

Told them of PD
Its importance to me
And couldn't they find me a ride?

"My daughter" said one
"May think it fun
To take you across" "No way, mother"
'I'll give you pounds ten'
"If that's the deal then
I'll take you myself" said the other

Was she for real?
'It's a deal, it's a deal'
Across on my way before six
Two hours daylight
Would see me alright
I was suddenly out of my fix

My heroine said
As she turned and led
Me down a steep path to the river
"Grab a couple of oars.
Here, this jacket's yours
Don't fall in or you'll certainly shiver"

Breath caught in my throat
As I thought 'Rowing boat!!'

And sure enough Kathryn stood there
Dragged her boat on a rope
Down the slippery slope
Sea breezes fanning her hair

Grabbed my rucksack
Threw it in the back
Helped me in the boat gently tossing
Proceeded to row
Half a mile or so
Back to the ferry boat crossing

Sun set in the sky
Mist drifts floated by
I was totally smitten – such bliss
"Please lean closer" she said
"We are up at the head"
I so wanted to give her a kiss

There was hardly a breeze
To rustle the trees
Only sound the rhythmical plop

Of oars in the water
I was thanking her daughter
And praying this moment won't stop

I asked 'May I row?'
Kathryn wisely said "No"
So I sat there and bathed in delight
Time didn't exist
As we floated on mist
With no other craft within sight

The trip had been magic
So I found it quite tragic
Too soon we reached the far side dock
All good things my friend
Must come to an end
Too soon I was back scrambling rocks

Recognition

If you're ever in Noss Mayo
Pop in for cream tea
And if you should see Kathryn
Please say hello for me

You'll surely find it easy
Kathryn to recognise
Tall, slim, blond hair flowing
Beautiful sea-green eyes

If earthly signs are not enough
Pray look for these instead
Wings sprouting from her shoulders
Shining circle round her head

Give Me a Break

Well after six and gathering fog might have made me tire
But still fantastic walking and my spirit was afire
On the headland turned to see Kathryn on her way
I pressed on to Wembury and thence to Heybrook Bay
With scenery exceptional I couldn't stop a grin
Occasionally chuckled to myself and even had a sing

At Eddystone Inn called it a day – dark and I was shattered
Two beers then taxi to Plymouth, light rain pitter-pattered
I'd covered 26 miles, faced frustrations but fought through
And I'd met my angel! Felt fantastic – wouldn't you?

Now Eurostar to Disney for 3-days of idle leisure
Meeting wife, daughter, grandkids – luxury and pleasure
I'd basically made Plymouth with my walk all but on track
Would do the 'missed' four miles just as soon as I got back

Confess that I was tempted to forget (don't tell my sister)
But knew I would regret it (see my novel Mister Blister)
No transport so walked both ways making it a little harder
Enjoyed Plymouth Breakwater and Drake awaiting the Armada

Cornwall

Crossed on the Cremyll ferry into Cornwall seeking sun

Keeping an eye for pirates down the barrel of a gun

Mount Edgecombe gardens had some truly horrendous bugs

A sign explained how leaving dog poo really is for mugs

Give Me a Sign

I've seen many signs use sarcasm and wit
"There's no Dog-Poo Fairy so bag your dog's shit"
They work, for I find in the remotest of places
Little evidence of failure: few traces of faeces

My boots are kept clean with pleasant fresh smell
'Steve, you have a dog so pray won't you tell
Why some dodgy dog owners are reluctant to do
The simplest of tasks – just bag up that poo?'

"When fresh it's runny, hot and steaming
Not the task of which you're dreaming
Ruins your walk when every day
Must scoop the poop and bag away"

Steve has the knack of changing your mind
You think you've been fair, he'll help you to find
A slant on the case you've not seen at all
Opens your eyes and makes you feel small

"I don't defend owners who simply won't do it
But try to persuade them that they shouldn't screw it
If walkers like you showed more care and respect
I'm sure fewer owners would act with neglect"

"When fresh it's runny, hot and steaming
Not the task of which you're dreaming
Ruins your walk when every day
Must scoop the poop and bag away"

But we both found most strange the new tendency
For dog poo filled bags to be hung on a tree
'It's an interesting stance – guess they think they win
With the pointless point scored: "I'll bag if you bin"'

Signs caused many a chuckle as I made my way
When naming their house did they mean to say
"Thank you" for what we'd agree is a lovely sight?
Parking sign looks selfish, claims it as their right
Greedy and pathetic with a very snooty air
"MY VIEW. ME, ME, ME, ME, ME. You go park elsewhere"

Bee Grateful

I'd heard much talk before my walk
Of fewer honey bees
They say this might cause terrible blight
Bring farming to its knees
So cheered when I saw along the shore

This ivy bush in flower

Bees buzzing around, flying insects abound
A shimmering living tower
Pollen for food to raise their brood
Helping recover their numbers
Fruit I remember well into November
Then holes for their winter slumbers

Missing Links

My T-shirt has a message on this course would be true
"It takes a lot of balls to golf the way I do"
Coastal courses very tough, often known as 'links'
Here the links are missing? Yes, 'missing links' methinks

The Gook

Great night in the pub in Portwrinkle
But made sure not to need a night tinkle
With this dreadful spook
Known as The Gook
Seeking lost balls – or a winkle?

Day	Start	End
29	West Bexington	Lyme Regis
30	Lyme Regis	Sidmouth
31	Sidmouth	Exmouth
32	Exmouth	Torquay
33	Torquay	Brixham
34	Brixham	Slapton
35	Slapton	Salcombe
36	Salcombe	Bigbury
37	Bigbury	Heybrook Bay
38	Heybrook Bay	Plymouth
39	Plymouth	Portwrinkle

Still Riding My Luck

Polperro late Sat afternoon
I started to look for a room
But they were all taken
So I'd burnt my bacon
Six miles more to Polruan

Thought 'My body and spirit are strong
It is mental where I'm going wrong'
Then met a strange pair
With hardly a care
Blissfully strolling along

"Tell me, sir, to where is your quest?"
'Polruan 'less I find nearer rest'
"Wow, that's a long way
Still, I bid you good day
We live just here, over this crest"

'Yes, must be four miles or so
Couldn't find anywhere in Polpero
I've got to rush on
Or the light will be gone
Unless *somewhere closer* you know'

"Well, you best get a real move on. See
That is our house and it's just time for tea"
'Yes, I'm really stuck
Down on my luck'
But both seemed quite dumb to my plea

'I'm desperate for SOMEWHERE TO SLEEP
Or I may end up cuddling sheep'
"Well, good luck mate"
'Did you hear? DES PER ATE'
"You must be – and from here the path's steep"

I gave up. They were stupid or cruel
And I wouldn't be anyone's fool
It's raining, I'm wet
I wouldn't beg – yet
"Oh you're walking for Parkinson's. Cool"

Reached edge of Polruan about eight
B&B, women chat at the gate
I am just sooo Jammy
'Mrs B? Mrs B?'
"We are but we're full. Hard luck mate"

"Your best bet's the ferry to Fowey
You might find the place a bit showy
But inns by the score
Along by the shore
Take care, though, it can be a bit blowy"

Down the hill and onto the craft
But the ferryman thought I was daft
"Any other night
Sure you'd be alright
Saturday Stags and Hens are on draft"

While inside and out gathered gloom
I trawled pubs and hotels for a room
Only offer: B&B
One hundred sixty!!
Seemed 'under the stars' was my doom

I followed the road up the hill
Dreaming of a comfy bed still
Found a nice friendly pub
Serving snacks and bar grub
Asked the barmaid 'a room?' with the bill

Couldn't get her to act fast, although
She kept saying "Landlady would know
Think her names Carol
I'll just change this barrel
Then ask her... in ten minutes or so"

The landlord, to my grateful elation
Found a room – Royal Inn near Par station
'I won't make a fuss
But I get there?' "By bus
Outside in ten mins" Jubilation!

Whole day had been muddle and mess
Still riding my luck to excess
I must plan ahead
Or could wind up dead
But I do like the challenge, confess

The coast didn't owe me a living
Show respect or it won't be forgiving
I was walking to test
My all-round fitness
But was taking too much and not giving

Best way back to Fowey: no fuss
Would have been on the very same bus
I came on last night
You've guessed it right
I missed it and boy did I cuss

Was my thinking becoming unstable?
Hadn't thought to check the timetable
Until the next morn
When I'd had my corn
Flakes and paid for my stable

When I got to the bus stop I saw
As I all but fell to the floor
It went at 8.10
I'd been eating then
The next was two hours and more

How had I been so stupid and thick
As to miss such a base, simple trick
After yesterday, too
This just wouldn't do
I must be getting mentally sick

The Saints Way

Decided to walk, yet again
Inflicting a physical pain
On my body to pay
For the Cavalier way
I was (not) using my brain

I found and thought I should try
A route used by folk better than I

Yes on the Saints Way
This sinner would pray
To the Great Path Spirit in the Sky

Extra miles and prayers made me late
Which now seemed my regular fate
So was in hurry
And starting to worry
Then met these folks just after a gate

Elspeth leant on Michael's shoulder
Which must have made me feel bolder
'Need help?' "No, we're fine
But my wife is quite blind
I'm her guide" (The Path Spirit's soldier?)

Their German Shepherd was called Jay
Guide dog but off duty that day
"We'll pose for a pic
But please take it quick"
We'll follow your walk blog all the way

Next day had my first major scare
As I strode along with my usual care
If I'd trod on this adder
I'd been sadder and madder
Wise up – you are driving me spare!'

Angel in Disguise

Approached Place Ferry feeling fine
Even better when I read this sign

so please take...
queue on pontoon, wait at top of steps for
instruction to board from ferry skipper.

TODAY'S SERVICE 18.9.12
TIDE STOP DUE TO VERY LOW
WATER! THERE WILL BE NO FERRY
@ 1345/1415/1445 SORRY
FOR ANY ISSUES! IF UNSURE
PLEASE CALL OFFICE ON NUMBER
above!!

Such a lucky chap
There before the gap
The day was turning out fine

Grinned as I walked to the shore
But mood shattered by what I saw
Ferry already leaving
The ferryman heaving
To push off his boat with an oar

I shouted but he simply waved
Started motor and went while I raved
Stuck here till past three
Is there no hope for me?
Then 'Perhaps my walk has been saved!'

I'd been rushing along every day
Now should enjoy my forced stay
This wasn't a pill
But gave time to chill
An important objective I'd say

So took a nap under some bowers
Then admired the plants and the flowers
To the boat – this won't do
Twenty-five in a queue!
'Oh no! I'll be stuck here for hours'

The first group went down at a pace
The ferryman then showed his face
"Someone waiting at 1.00?
Was it you my old son?
Come on, I've saved you a place"

Wow! Perhaps I had misjudged this guy?
He had saved me a seat but still why
Had he left me before
Stuck on the shore?
"I guess you saw I was high and dry?"

"When I came over at one o'clock
Trust me it was quite a shock
So low was the tide
Despite how I tried
I found that I just couldn't dock"

"Ran aground, poled off with my oar
Took the passengers back as you saw
To whence they came
St Mawes is its name
But now I'm back here once more"

Oh boy I felt such a fool
Selfish, narrow-minded and small
Giving others the blame
For my own failings – shame!
While this man was a star and so cool

"With tides so extreme though we try
Can't predict quite how low nor how dry
St Mawes' harbour wall
Is thirty feet tall
But may well be topped by the high"

That wasn't the only thing he taught me

Angels, Angels Everywhere

When wishing to cross a bog, wetland or stream
Stepping stones can be useful, save choosing between
Walk upstream to a bridge – waste both time and feet
If its deep, you can swim – may drown (don't tell Pete)
Shallow? Just wade in, first take off boots and socks
Hope current not strong, no glass or sharp rocks

But the stones can be slippery – fall in with a curse
Results in a soaking but often times worse
So was very impressed to find these were so clean
Unusually clear of weed – not dread 'wet and green'

The question was answered: it was two likely lads
Using brushes to clean them which made me feel glad
Yet one more thankless task done on our behalf
By our coastal councils and their cheerful, helpful staff

Turning Points and Land Marks

The Lizard. Furthest south on mainland GB
Foggy wet day but huge milestone for me
Most south-east and most south, that's 2 out of 8
Land's End will make 3 so let's go, I can't wait

Stranger Danger

Below is just one of the path's hidden dangers
From the 'wrong' side could be curtains for strangers
Unseen erosion, slight carelessness here
Stand near the edge to look down and – oh dear!

St Michael's Mount – another landmark
Traditional point for pilgrims to embark
Via France to Spain's Santiago de Compostela
All on your knees – if you're that kind of fellah

Came across this statue on the front at Penzance
Fantastic – just check out the focus and stance

Depicting a rescue from shore to sea
By throwing a line, which is rather tricky
So whenever you're asked to Lifeboats donate
Give loads of cash – who knows what's their fate?

After less than two months I'd arrived at Land's End
World famous landmark, now I'm round the bend
Head up the west coast then to John O'Groats
Doesn't sound very far when written in notes
Seven months on footpaths following the coast
Had my photo taken, gave myself a toast

I was clearly far fitter than I'd ever been
Everything was better than I'd dared to dream
Deserved to put my feet up for a moment's rest

As did a young thatcher like me in mid-quest
Equalling my pleasure and self-fulfilment thrill
Next generation craftsman sharpening his skill

Cornwall is famed for clapper bridges and tin mines
I recalled a Mister Blister poem from summer '99

When first I set my eyes on Geevor Mine
I felt its peaceful power; a silent shrine
To men who gave their lives to mining tin
Drilling. Blasting. Crushing. Shaking. DIN

Iron balls were used for crushing rocks
Hewn by men well used to taking knocks
But now tin's price on global markets falls
Out comes the man from London with no balls

'We have to close the mine' turns to depart
Iron headed man, with iron heart

Walking to raise money and awareness of PD
Many living with it would just love to have been me
Wondered would some be upset or even take offence
Think I was showing off my fitness at their expense
These thoughts in a Zennor pub resulted in this ballad
(OK for something written over a pint and blue cheese salad)

Get one in for Parki
Don't let him be forgot
Remember all the good times
And everything you've got

Yes, get one in for Parki
He'd love to join you there
Or better still go fetch him
He's waiting in his chair

So, get one in for Parki
He'd be there, yes its true
Remember your turns coming
Will they get one in for you?

Also thought of Tom Isaacs who ten years before me
Had walked the GB Coast while suffering from PD
On return he had set up the Cure Parkinson's Trust
Raising millions for the cause "cos find a cure we must"
Zany sense of humour, may say "T'was just a stroll"
The truth is in his great book titled: 'Shake, Rattle and Roll'
If forced to write a poem (I think he prefers prose)
May be more like this one – if not treading on his toes:

It makes you shake and shuffle
And feel a little flat
When someone says
"Get that down you – no,
I didn't mean like that!'

Hayle and Hearty Campervan Man

St Ives with tide so far out that the harbour was quite dry

Me too! On to Hayle with an ice cream – gulls, don't even try!

WARNING

SEAGULLS CAN ATTACK
TO STEAL FOOD
EATEN OUTSIDE

KEEP YOUR FOOD
WELL SHIELDED

PUBLIC AWARENESS NOTICE ISSUED BY
ST IVES TOWN COUNCIL

The Towans is fantastic, just look at that sand
Wildlife spotting in the dunes nestled close at hand

Lynn was at Gwithian with our new campervan!!
Bought from Stuart Jessup another coast walk man

He and dog Poppy walked England's coast and raised a wealth
Of money for and awareness of his cause Mental Health
I'd spent a half day with him near his finish in the summer
And he'd been very generous to this coast walking newcomer
Gave me spreadsheets of his route including daily miles
Bus routes, timetables "Save you time" modestly he smiles
"Coasters must stick together, I'll help every way I can"
Little did he suspect that I'd end up with his van!

A Campervan! My world an even more wonderful place

Scooted along the clifftops a broad smile upon my face

Tide very low so fine beach as I approached Portreath

Deep in tin mine country – wonder what lies beneath

Old mines can be death traps but here they had it right
Cage to stop brats falling in but let bats out at night

Came across these wise old birds, known as Cornish Chough
Almost always seen in threes, are two not tough enough?

Month 2 Review

I'd so enjoyed the first two months
The scenery and weather
Flora, fauna, history
Everything together

Physical pleasant surprise
Spirit top of the tree
The only part that bothered was
My own mentality

Decided to reward myself
For hitting two of three
Yes, I think you've guessed it
'Cornish cream tea for me!'

Don't want to end my days like this

Tumbling to the shore
Keep focused on the task ahead
Whatever was in store

I'd thought 'Mental' would be my strength
I better think some more!

Day	Start	End
40	Portwrinkle	Fowey
41	Fowey	Mevagissey
42	Mevagissey	Carne Beach
43	Carne Beach	Gyllyngvase Beach
44	Gyllyngvase Beach	Coverack
45	Coverack	Lizard
46	Lizard	Praa Sands
47	Praa Sands	Porth Curno
48	Porth Curno	Zennor
49	Zennor	Gwithian
50	Gwithian	Holywell
51	Holywell	Porthcothan

October 2012

Witch Craft

The Fall

October and the days were drawing in
But I was happy and the sun still shone
Fantastic scenery and I hadn't a care
Until, that is, I looked over there
And suddenly thought 'I could be gone'

You could stroll along with no idea
Of what was or wasn't below you
Suddenly a gap beneath your feet
You're doing an Alice, no time to tweet
And it's "Was nice to know you"

Reflections

Stunning views if you kept your eyes up
Enjoying cliffs, beach, sky and sea
Walkers passing now and again
Surfers seeking a perfect ten
But not a one happy as me

And now a perfect rock pool brought
Instant reflections of my youth
In 'The Perishers' Daily Mirror cartoon
Boot the dog made the chief crabs swoon
When he came seeking the pond life truth

For every summer on his holiday
Boot stuck his face into the water
The crabs saw an omen from the sky
Read into it signs of dread days nigh
When like us they shouldn't oughter

Fascinating to think of tiny creatures
Enjoying their lives as best they can
Oblivious to weirdos like me
Who day after day plod by the sea
To finish back where they began

While life goes on for normal folk
Working at their nine to five
Unless they're on a life-boat crew
Donning gear as down she flew
Helping keep sailors alive

Just What the Doctor Ordered

Approaching Padstow surprised and pleased
To come across a cheering sign

'October now, expect it's closed'
But no. I found perfect repose
Toasted tea cakes, just sublime

Excessive rain for many weeks
Had left the path one endless puddle
Slippery mud water on top
Feared Doctor Foster's awful plop
Stepping in up to my muddle

Required close attention to avoid
Slipping straight over the side
Or grabbing barbed wire once again
Slitting my wrist with serious pain
Solution: walk one foot each side

Again I hummed my wet day song
Paul Simon's 'Slip Sliding Away'
Port Isaac came into view
Expect the name's not new to you
'Doc Martin' wasn't in that day

But series fans may recognise
Doc Martin's surgery and the school

While I soon had another care
Chased by cows with dodgy stare
I struggled to maintain my cool

I scooted down a ten foot drop
Which they seemed wary of descending
But noticed some were going round
To cut me off from safer ground
Was I to have a hoofy ending?

To give myself feeble defence
I took my rucksack from my back
But they came faster all the while
I vaulted over a nearby stile
I eyed them – they eyed me back!

Ruined Castles

Tintagel, King Arthur and Knights
Of the famed Round Table
Magician Merlin, Guinivere
Loyal Launcelot all lived here
And will again – so goes the fable

But now a place I must forget
My worries: crazy cows no more!
Boscastle whose harbour brought fame
Its tangled streets and witchcraft claim
Torn by floods August 2004

In our cosy homes we watched the water
Thunder down their street
Harbour strewn with tangled cars
Bridges and houses bore the scars
But Boscastle would not accept defeat

Weeks, months, years of rebuilding
Homes, businesses and lives
Unlike Tintagel which must wait
For Arthur to fulfil its fate
Now once again Boscastle thrives

Eavesdropping

Could tell you where and what this is
But then I'd have to kill you

So hark instead the shreiks of mirth
As children learn to ride the surf
Which certainly can thrill you

Logistics

As summer goes the campsites close
Hostels and B&B's too
You know my plan I'd bought a van
With kitchen, sink, shower and loo

Places to store clothes, food and more
Warm bed – snug as a bug
Much better bet than cold and wet
In a tent I'd have to lug

It was just great to vegetate
After a hard day's walk
Then cook my dinner (still getting thinner)
And listen to radio talk

Wash and clean note where I'd been
My Facebook blog to write
Relaxed and fed so make my bed
And kiss myself goodnight

But I'm sure you see as well as me
I was in a bit of a fix
Having walked all day the van's miles away
Solution: logistics

So every night till my head flops
I'm comparing routes, bus times and stops
Checking mileage, tides and places
Would my plan keep up my paces?
Just when I thought I was mentally fit
This factual farce comes and spoils it

Drive to the start, lock van, depart
Go freely on my way
Walk 'til I drop find a bus stop
And catch it back. OK?

Bus stops are rare not everywhere
Especially on the coast
I had to change and rearrange
To try to make the most

For peace of mind I had to find
Whenever I was able
A parking place adjust my pace
To fit the bus timetable

To avoid a wreck I'd have to check
Which route and times were best
Rather a chore and a bit of a bore
But all part of the test

Bus routes are many, buses few if any
But don't give in to sorrow
I'll be all right, I've got all night
To sort it for tomorrow

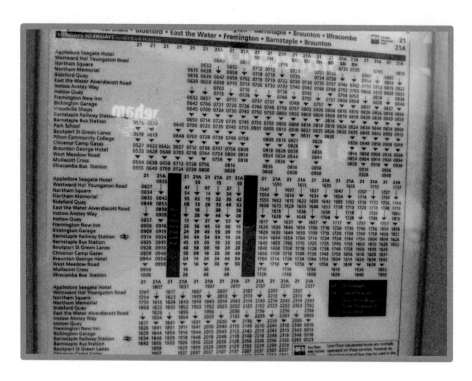

For every night till my head flops
I'm comparing routes, bus times and stops
Checking mileage, tides and places
Would my plan keep up my paces?
Just when I thought I was mentally fit
This factual farce comes and spoils it

Networks complex so sure to vex
Could really be a swine
My biggest friend a real godsend
Was the bus timetable on line

Add to the fun rather than one
More choices I'm afraid
Drive, bus or walk first? (The last is worst
In case you get delayed)

"It seems to me its 2 times 3"
6 options – I can't take it
With routes and times and parking fines
And am I sure I'll make it?!

Hold on a sec just want to check
The ways to solve the riddle
Thinking it through there are 2 times 2
Let me show you the fiddle

Park – walk – ride: best check the tide
Walk – ride – drive: if still alive
Park – ride – walk: does the timetable talk?
Ride – walk – drive: next would be five!

But ride – drive – walk or walk – drive – ride
Just don't work out, trust me, I've tried
With these combos, when you arrive
There's no van there for you to drive!

I want to relax but with all these facts
Spinning in my head
No time to eat, to nurse my feet
Nor catch zzzz's in my bed

'Cos every night till my head flops
I'm comparing routes, bus times and stops
Checking mileage, tides and places
Will my plan keep up my paces?
Just when I thought I was mentally fit
This factual farce comes and spoils it

How NOT To Do It

At Mouth Mill the stream, often asleep
Was rain-swollen so fast and deep

A group coming the other way
Were well prepared I have to say
With sticks and wellies to their knees
They made the crossing at their ease

I praised their efforts, keen and zealous
Hiding the fact that I was jealous
Tried to look as cool as they
As if I walked miles every day!!
Started to cross leggings in socks
Trying to stand on green / wet rocks

I slipped and slid, got many a booty
Sticking to my 'pro' walker's duty
But it was soon plain to us all
That I was heading for a fall
So sat mid-stream on prominent rocks
Took off my leggings, boots and socks

Leggings and socks now stuffed in boots
Set off again – mid cheers and hoots
I hadn't taken the care I oughter
A legging was floating off down water
A forlorn chase but amazing luck
On a driftwood raft my legging stuck

Grabbed it and made the other side
Chuckling, not to cover my pride
But because it always makes me laugh
When I try to be clever but act so daft
That it all goes wrong and I look a fool
Can't help but giggle, just can't be cool

Lovelly Clovelly

Built round a street cobbled and steep
Which YOU can ride on donkey or jeep
(Note, dear reader, there's no way
I sneaked a donkey ride that day)
But pirates climbed to rape and pillage
Clovelly's a lovely harboured village

From Clovelly headed for Westward Ho!
Along a carriage drive you go
Fed up with boots wore for a change
Light trainers from my footwear range
At the time it seemed a good idea
Forgot how wet it was that year

Rock of Ages

Fantastic rock formations clearly show
What any schoolkid now would surely know
These rocks were formed in layers over ages
As sediment deposits built in stages
Forced into curves and ridges by the stresses
As one tectonic plate against another presses

The Rock spoke to me: "It's ludicrous, absurd
For religious leaders reading from 'The Word'
To claim 'Creation took less than a week
About six thousand years ago' or shriek
'In His own image man God did create
Then realised he'd need a mate to mate

So from a spare rib next created Eve'
The sexism could really make you heave
'A snake persuaded Eve to get her mate
To eat an apple; God threw them out the gate
Of Eden bcause that fruit was off the menu
Adam and Eve had to find another venue'

'To punish his creation's poor behaviour
God drowned them all, except for Noah the saviour
And his kin so they could start again
His Ark contained two of each animal strain'
Sunday school is where they start these lies
Adult listeners like you should be too wise

To keep you in the dark they hid the truth
Knowing what they preached was without proof
'The Sun goes round the Earth, with Hell below'
And when proved wrong by such as Galileo
Threatened them with torture on the wrack
Unless they took their blasphemous words back

'Show the Love of God' their stated aim
Despised and killed others who said the same
'True knowledge comes to us from God's own book'
Burnt 'witches', hated gays and racist took
Babies of 'heathen' mothers into 'care'
To be abused by priests and nuns in there

Slowly they adapt their claims and acts
To fit the modern world and science facts
Gay marriage, female priests, there's no Limbo
Now Heaven's not above, nor Hell below
Now Hell does not exist: torture, torment
Cannot a loving Father represent

'Original Sin' church code for 'having sex'
Without it humanity would soon be 'ex'!
Christ didn't come to Earth your sins to bear
Such illogical nonsense just doesn't wear
If 'God' wanted to forgive he could just do it
Create then sacrifice a son? unnecessary to it!

My words can help tackle the human crisis
Of new religious zealots such as ISIS
If there's one thing you learn from your trip
Make it 'don't fall for such MisLeadership'
Refute religious leaders' rants and rages
Learn the lessons from the Rock of Ages"

A main objective of my walk for me
Was developing my spiritual clarity
The Rock's words made me feel 'I'm getting there'
But may be stuff for which you do not care
So I promise here to focus on the walking
The Rock speaks for itself, I cannot stop it talking

The Lovely Lyns

Lynmouth / Lynton full of good cheer
The imaginative models shown here
Are all in one garden
Beg the owner's pardon
(If he finds out I'm buying his beer)

Done viewing headed for the gate
Would have stayed but was getting late
Last model was best
Check my manly chest
Disappointed I'd not lost more weight

The cliff railway to Lynton is great
Water pumped at the top gives the weight
To lift the car up the track
Then send it right back
Water out, water in, close the gate

If you're down Exmoor or North Devon way
And you're looking for somewhere to stay
Try one of the Lyns
Sure to bring grins
At the end of your sightseeing day

Valley of Rocks

Fantastic place, Valley of Rocks
But the views included some shocks
My eyes need to wake up
Ponies wearing make-up?
And combed each others flowing locks?!

It's two months that I've been away
But if starting to see ponies that way

I need contemplation
And for meditiation
Can't beat this view down to Lee Bay

The scenery's fantastic must say
Hills, woods and streams all the way
Beaches, waterfalls
Yes this stretch has it all

Talking trees? Sure, I heard this one neigh!

Pride Comes Before a Fall

I'd reached the end of the SWCP
650 miles covered comfortably
I'd assumed it might be the toughest bit
So confidence high I felt totally fit
The sculpture's excellent inspiration and style
Quality, relevant, brings forth a smile
Recalling the one that I'd seen at the start
Certainly quickened the beat of my heart

No peace for the wicked, at least not for me
OK, so I'd finished the SWCP
Couldn't let that triumph go to Minehead
Had a couple of beers, then to myself said
Where one path finishes another's beget
So best foot forward into West Zumerzet

Minehead beach a doddle, quality sand
Sunny day, morale high still feeling grand
Relaxed as I strolled no care in the world
Admiring the banners of Butlin's unfurled
Up from the beach was an innocent ramp
Families used to and from Butlin's camp

But not going there I stepped off the side
Onto firm looking sand and suddenly cried
Leg went straight through and dangled in space
Fell on my other knee, stomach and face
Rocks used as a breakwater and ramp support
Had been covered in wind-blown sand they had caught

Said a women who'd seen my impromptu show
"Happened to my husband just two weeks ago"
Tweeted council and Butlin's, received no reply
So hope all their clients are as lucky as I
For weeks taken care of the dangers around
Nigh broke my leg on smooth sandy 'safe' ground

WATCHET!!

This fantastic statue celebrates a poet
Much better than me, no don't argue, I know it
Inspired by a visit to Watchet in his time
Sam Coleridge had written his poem "The Rime
Of The Ancient Mariner" which is special you see
To both me and the sailor who sat watching me

Tried steps to the beach but the previous day
During a bad storm they'd been swept clean away
I managed to scramble down the cliff face
To find myself in a strange marvellous place

Fantastic cliff patterns, beach of crazy paving

But after four miles a way up I was craving
Tide coming in my nerves getting frayed

Phew! A ladder to heaven and very well made
I hadn't feared drowning but wanted to try
Avoiding a rescue by the RNLI

I climbed to the top and did nothing but stare
This fantastic fossil was just lying there

Collecting fossils

- Cliffs and beaches near East Quantoxhead and Kilve are part of the "Lilstock to Blue Anchor" geological SSSI, and also part of the Quantock Area of Outstanding Natural Beauty. It is extremely important that they are not damaged by fossil hunters.

- Fossils must only be taken when they are loose from the rocks. Only collect on the lower beaches where the sea has washed away clay and mud.

- Do not collect from or hammer into the cliffs, embedded fossils or rocky ledges.

- Keep collecting to a minimum and don't remove any fixed fossils or other rocks or minerals.

- The collection of actual specimens should be restricted to those places where there is a plentiful supply.

- Only collect souvenirs ..... leave something for others. These fossils are part of everybody's heritage.

- Be considerate and never do anything which leaves a site in an unsightly or dangerous condition.

- Remember that collecting fossils for sale is illegal.

- The fossils are the property of the East Quantoxhead Trust. Taking fossils in contravention of this notice will be regarded as theft.

Walked up some lanes to Kilve and found its pub
The landlord said "We're famous for our grub
The village hall has parking for the night
Some pints of Doom Bar will then set you right
First catch the bus it stops here right outside"
I took up his suggestions and went for the ride
Picked up CV and was back by half past seven
Armchair, log fire, pint and meal – pure heaven
Did my planning over a pint of Doom Bar ale
Given all the recent rain how was the Parrett Trail?

Day	Start	End
52	Porthcothan	Padstow
53	Padstow	Port Isaac
54	Port Isaac	Boscastle
55	Boscastle	Bude
56	Bude	Hartland Quay
57	Clovelly	Hartland Quay
58	Appledore	Westward Ho!
59	Clovelly	Westward Ho!
60	Braunton	Instow
61	Woolacombe	Braunton
62	Woolacombe	Coombe Martin
63	Lynton	Coombe Martin
64	Porlock Weir	Lynton
65	Porlock Weir	Minehead
66	Minehead	Kilve

River Parrett Trail Tale

Next morning, when I'd parked CV I saw an EA truck
Thought I'd ask the men inside if I'd have much luck
Knew I'd made a bad mistake when my opening 'Hi
I'm walking the River Parrett Trail' received the dumb reply
"I'm sitting in a car" 'is it flooded do you know?'
"If it was I'd get out". I decided time to go

SOMERSETSHIRE DRAINAGE ACT 1877

NOTICE IS HEREBY GIVEN THAT ANY PERSON OR PERSONS FOUND REMOVING SAND OR SHINGLE OR IN ANY WAY INTERFERING WITH OR DAMAGING THE SEA DEFENCES WILL BE PROSECUTED

BY ORDER
GEORGE LOVIBOND
DATED COMMISSIONERS OFFICE
BRIDGWATER NOVEMBER 1886
CLERK TO THE SOMERSETSHIRE DRAINAGE COMMISSIONERS

In actual fact the R P trail was springy grass and dry
Winding atop flood barriers, built both broad and high
At the coast the tide was out so I had a perfect view
Whirlpools carved in solid rock back a million years or two

Next day a more sensible Environment Agency guy
Agreed to take my photo – I pretended to be shy
Look too like the knotted hankie man from Monty Python
Only difference I can see: my knotted hankie's gone

Closing in on Wales

Burnham-on-Sea miles of mud flats beyond the sandy beach
Warning signs of 'stick in the mud's say don't go out of reach

Burnham, Berrow, Brean, Brean Down on and on and on

At last the headland gives a view of Super-Mare (Weston)

Where I took a weekend off, my foot off of the throttle
And my lovely line dance friends gave me a hot water bottle

We visited a local town, they said I looked too slim
So popped into St John's fine church to pray for this pilgrim

So impressed by Clevedon Pier its seen some sights no doubt

Imagine 50 feet of water twice daily in and out

Housing boom on waste ground near famous Portbury Dock
With strangest guard dog ever seen on duty round the clock

It was nearly four o'clock and I was in a fix
Having nine miles more to go and dark soon after six
M5 to cross the river Avon hoping I could reach
Where I'd left CV that morn, the misnamed Severn Beach
I thought I'd judged it to a T as I jogged the final mile
But when I spied these footballers couldn't help but smile

Welsh Wales

Next day would be a special one, a real landmark I reckoned
Having walked ten weeks or more another country beckoned
England goodbye, with glint in eye
Wales would be my second

I'd be crossing the river Severn heading into Wales
Keen to walk its new coast path, learn its lore and tales
Meet a dragon that sings, fire-breathing, huge wings
with shining golden scales

Searching for a safe crossing to keep Peter content
The M4 has no walking path so up the coast I went
The M48 has one and is much more fun
So I crossed toward Cas-Gwent

Overnight in a Peterstone Wentlooge pub car park
Then 7.20 Newport bus to find something quite dark
Sculptures in pain which the pouring rain
Made extra strange and stark

Time for tea and toast before meeting Hugh Coombes
Twenty years work mate and friend, now here he looms
No, it's a troll! Quick find a hole
Or we've both met our dooms

I'd assumed stroll to P W, lunch, pick up CV
Drive Hugh back to Newport or wherever he need be
But Hugh just smiles "Cardiff's 20 miles
That sounds good to me"

He'd arranged to meet his wife there at 5.15 approx
"Eight hours is plenty of time if we pull up our socks"
Say 'That may be too far for me'?
I couldn't bear the mocks

Slapped him on his back and 'Yeah, that's great' I said
Done extra miles last few days and my feet felt like lead
But with this pain a day I'd gain
which I could spend in bed

Through town to path Hugh shot off at a tremendous pace
Jolted from my steady stride I struggled to keep place
Two miles go by I'm forced to cry
'Woah, man, it's not a race'

We slowed to a pleasant stroll – Hugh still made the going
Until I heard a curve-horned bull for calf and heifer lowing
Yelled in Hugh's ear 'I'm out of here'
My two clean heels were showing

Hugh was carrying a large rucksack yet didn't make a fuss
I wondered what he had in there but couldn't seem to sus
Make no mistake it was full of cake
And drinks for both of us

"Wales CP's too new for books. Downloaded 20 pages"
Knew local history, characters, kept me enthralled for ages
Then started to flag and his right foot drag
One of my favourite stages

In Cardiff knew all the pubs, chose one by the bus station
Insisted on buying all the beers and gave me a donation
I sure like Hugh and you would too
– a credit to his nation

Bus back to Peterstone's Six Bells and ate a massive steak
Followed by enormous slice of double choc fudge cake
A local band took to the stand
And made the rafters shake

Nos Da Studio, Cardiff had a room that sounded right
Warm and friendly, all needs met, guaranteed few fights
And a lie this ain't, live models to paint!!
But only Thursday nights

First thing I did to wide acclaim (I'd noticed people cower)
Though keen to start my walking day was run myself a shower
Off came the grime, sweat and slime
It took but half an hour

To the station to catch a train, feeling keen and pure
Walking back from Barry Island if I could resist the lure
But such is fate, two years too late
For the Gavin and Stacey tour

Great fish and chips too long to cook and it was after one
I'd done it again, got behind time relaxing, having fun
When I start slow things seem to go
Downhill at a run

Fortunately a short walk day only 12 miles to do
Three miles an hour, done by five, nearly dark I knew
So off I went with good intent
But rather wary too

A Fence Offence

I really chuckled at this sign, my thoughts to a T
Such good land fenced off and wasted angers me
More so when seems more miles it means
Cry Freedom! Liberty!

OK someone might fall in, maybe even drown
But can't let this nanny state mamby pamby around
Kids need to dare, become aware
For hidden risks abound

Once world's largest coal port, scale was immense
Now their wide smooth water's cut off by a fence
No water sports, you spoil ports
Of course, no recompense

Local kids with nowt to do can see this lost resource
Initial calm frustration grows to anger in due course
The real danger, to this stranger
Boredom and drugs of course

Followed a dock road through for let us say two miles
Huge locked gates huge watchmen wearing huge false smiles
"No footpath now, got lost somehow"
Another of my trials

Tried my "Walking for PD" but they ignored my pleading
'I will have to go right back' but found a side path leading
Passed a pile of logs and two guard dogs
Luckily they weren't feeding!

Though the extra fun and games compounded my late start
Lavernock Point's broad grass strip cheered my aching heart
And I knew in town lights all around
Would play a useful part

Last Saturday in October and swiftly night drew in
Saw a girl in 'fancy dress?' She answered with a grin
"Why? What you saying? Best start praying
Or I'll drink your blood like gin"

Looked like she had stuff to do, get Dracula to marry her?
White face so she needed blood, I hadn't time to carry her
Welsh Assembly Hall looked very cool
Across the Cardiff Bay Barrier

HARD STEPS

Cliffs at Rhoose Point with curved white beach before
Astonishing wall of pebbles stretched along the shore
But happily sand along the strand
Saved my feet once more

Train crossed on a viaduct over wooded valley and stream

Signs warned beware of falling rocks, images extreme

Was well aware I must take care
Or a sad end to my dream

Enchanting stream meandering beside salt marsh and pool

Next thing, BANG, flat on my back after a nasty fall
Rubbed my arm but no real harm
Except felt such a fool

Day dreaming down these steps and I hadn't seen
That, as on the Isle of Wight, they were wet and green
Boots had slipped, I had tipped
This path can be so mean

Can't claim I like to wear it but I've found my rucksack
Breaks my fall and thus protects my poor old aching back
But its still a shock when I hit a rock
With a resounding smack

Entered the seawatch centre feeling quite shook up
Manned by a woman who welcomed me, offering a cup
Of hot sweet tea while she told me
The facts. I lapped them up

We chatted for a good half hour about all things marine
Atmospheric and nautical, she was extremely keen
Didn't laugh or create 'bout my muddy state
Perhaps she hadn't seen

Riding My Luck

Sadly tempus was fugiting so I limped off on my way
Still hoping for an early end to another long tough day
There's an early bus don't make a fuss
Just hobble quickly and pray

Col-hum Point had good surfing, its cafe offered stew
Placed a Pavlovian order and spoke to a couple who
Saw me weeks back at Coverack
So we chatted over a brew

Back on earth the stew arrived, recalled the early bus!!
Take it slow and catch the next? 'NO!' (said with a cuss)
Bolted the stew and off I flew
The early one or bust!

Half-jogged mile to St Donat's made me come alive
Squeezed by over-tight kissing gate, leaving minutes five
Ran to the end and round the bend
Saw the bus arrive!

Drove CV to all-year site on Porthcawl's outer road
But was no reception sign and not a light there glowed
Another man in another van
His preparedness showed

"Sopping wet but ten pitches, just two occupied
Gravel path to start with, then grass on either side"
That's all he said, then in he sped
The mud soon stopped his ride

How lucky was I? (how lucky I'd been so far on this trip)
If h'ed not gone rushing in I'd have been for the slip
Though chance was low I tried to tow
But couldn't get the grip

He decided (wise choice I thought) "Stay here for the night
Ring the owner in the morn and sort it in the light
Given the dark I decided to park
On tarmac outside. Goodnight

Cooked / ate meal, washed up, showered, even used the loo
Slept like a log then scooted off scot free into the blue
The guy still stuck, I thought 'Good luck
Getting off that goo'

I'd set an alarm to ensure I caught the 7.50 bus
Porthcawl to Bridgend thence St Donat's 9.30 no fuss
Had toast and jam and then thought damn
I've cut it fine (worse cuss)

Very late nowhere to park and where does my bus stop?
Had given up but one last try, up here behind this shop
There's a space! Big grin on face
Still might end on top

Rammed feet in boots, grabbed my bag, ran to the crossroad
The bus was coming the other way, I'm such a jammy toad
"Hello my friend" 'Single Bridgend'
Sat down and all but crowed

The shale nature of the rock means some sections wearing
Quicker than their neighbours do, leaving huge gaps glaring
So keep away or some fine day
To the beach you may be tearing

The Pelican in Her Piety is quite a name for a pub
But it served a good strong ale and wide range of quality grub
Prawn baguette was what I ate
But can you guess the rub?

'Another pint young serving wench' when she brought it back
'Where can I cross the river' "Just down the opposite track
Are stepping stones" now hear my groans
"But the tide is passed the slack"

I had the gall to curse my luck as I drank in the pain
But I'm so dumb – this morning's bus! now no thinking again!
Necked the beer, note to self here:
'Please start to use your brain'

The stepping stones were obvious – as was the dodgy gap
Green, wet, submerged or missing – I gave myself a slap
'Fair payback for your stupid lack
Of planning, which is crap'

I survived with one bootie and a slip on the next stone
When I thought I was a goner but hung on with a moan
Made it, felt smug then stupid mug
As I spied with a groan

A sign on this side pointing out a footbridge just up stream
I could have safely strolled over, what a wally I had been
I'd risked a fall which could ruin all
My health, my walk, my dream

Even if I hadn't hurt myself I would have been soaked through
Still had about five miles to go and as I surely knew
Had I fallen in with a sharp, cold wind
I'd have been frozen blue

Rising Spirits

I found a site, Happy Valley, which sounded worth a try
Arrived to find reception closed but club house warm and dry
The guy in there was more than fair
"Sausage, egg and chips I'll fry"

"Pour you a pint then ring the owners, see what they suggest
We're closed to tourers but you seem to really need a rest
You'll want a shower, here's a coin for power"
Yes I was sure impressed

The owners said "The field's so wet that its more like the sea
But please park near the office and use the facilities free"
Excellent! With heart content
'OK' said gratefully

A comfortable night but yet more rain and a storm of hail
With path so muddy, gear so wet, began to think I'd fail
Forced a smile 'Part of the trial
You didn't want plain sail'

Another wet and windy day, by the time I reached Porthcawl

227

Stiff and cold but at a coffee house right on the sea wall
"Coffee + cake?" 'Yes, I'll partake'
Then to CV did crawl

At Happy Valley pleased to find there was a Halloween do
I was invited so had a shave and put on my best gear too
The meal was free, they spoiled me
But I was feeling blue

Midnight came and midnight went, people started to leave
I was watching for an angel in which I could believe
Black or White magic for though it sounds tragic
I'd nothing up my sleeve

I shuffled back to CV, silent sad cold place of rest
Alone as a lonesome spirit seeking its lone life quest
Shivered there in the dark with low life spark
My heart cold in my chest

At Halloween as we all know there are spirits everywhere
Witches and warlocks on broomsticks flying through the air
The rain poured down, prayed they wouldn't drown
Nor my spirit as I lay there

I don't believe in Good and Bad, nor simple Black and White
We are each home to a spirit doing whatever it feels right
So I made my toast 'Every spirit or ghost'
And bade 'All Souls Good Night'

Month three was over, finished, but straight in to number four
Walk suddenly felt endless: endless coast round endless shore
Clung to what I knew: if I fought through
Winter hols after one month more

Day	Start	End
67	Bridgwater	Kilve
68	Bridgwater	Brean Sands
69	Brean Sands	Clevedon
70	Sandy Bay	Weston Super Mere
71	Clevedon	Severn Beach
72	Severn Beach	Severn Tunnel Junct
73	Severn Tunnel J	Newport
74	Newport	Cardiff
75	Barry Island	Cardiff
76	Barry Island	St Donat's
77	St Donat's	Porthcawl
78	Baglan	Porthcawl

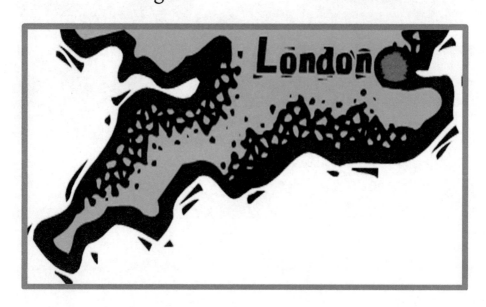

November 2012

WHY?!

Close Shave

Hail all night but was alright
Snug and warm in my lovely CV
Usual jumbles, drove to The Mumbles
Then the bus back to Port T
Underestimated power
Of Swansea's rush hour
Which almost did for me

Late for the bus, started to cuss
Where's a parking space
That will do, off with shoes
Then a smile found my face
I sang a song for the bus came along
As I was doing up my lace

The tide about a mile out
When I reached Swansea Bay
Without a toss I cut across
It seemed the fastest way
"Want some live bait?" but I couldn't wait
The sky more black than grey

With a skip and a hop made Lido's tea shop
As the storm began to bellow
To celebrate a hot chocolate
Whipped cream topped marshmallow
Rain pelted down I saw with a frown
'Could do with a haircut old fellow'

Silver Lining

I'd promised Parki I'd get round GB
'Will be a piece of cake'
But I still had nigh a month 'fore I
Reached even my winter break
And as you know I'd been feeling low
Struggling and no mistake

I'd had my meal started to feel
My e-mails I should check
Opened one up, near dropped my cup
As I shouted 'flipping heck
That's the best, beats all the rest'
A load fell from my neck

"You don't know me but as you'll see
My son gave your address
My hubbie's a walker – I'm more of a talker
And if you'll be our guest
I'll cook your dinner, our bed's a winner
I think I can confess"

"Checked your dates and at this rate
Mwnt's November 26
If you care he'll meet you there
Details we can fix
Walk four days – he knows the ways
So you can just take pics"

"Then each night if it's alright
And doesn't mean a fuss
Dinner B&B without a fee
You can stay with us
I'll drive the car to where you are
Much better than the bus"

Tear in my eye wrote my reply
Fantastic silver lining
A chink of light glowing bright
Through my clouds was shining
Yet again when feeling pain
An Angel relieved my pining

The sun came out, without a doubt
Everything seemed brighter
Birds were singing churchbells ringing
Even my bag felt lighter
My spirit rose I was on my toes
Feeling like a fighter

Merry Meetings

At Threecliff Bay the tide was so far out
I walked the beach round Great Tor with no doubt
Three miles of sand to the café on Oxwich Beach
Which was indeed a pleasant place to reach
Pearl gave a bacon roll and pot of tea
Other customers £7 for my charity

My sister, nephew, mum and Lynn met me
While touring round Gower and Rhossili
Worms Head the tide too high to cross that day
So carried on along Rhossili Bay

Felt safe entering this wood, bright and green

But saw the strangest bird I'd ever seen

Parkinson's UK Pwll group had arranged a talk
For me to tell their members all about my walk
Was scheduled to speak from 2.00 to 2.30
But then chatted and drank til after 3.00
Which left six miles to Loughor Castle and van
Last two very dark... but cycle path, lucky man

Great Parking Spot

Decided drive CV to Carmarthon
Find quiet place to park – shouldn't take long
For no special reason try Tre-gynwr
No Sat Nav, lost in town so 'Check map here'
Up steep hill side road happily spied
Road with high blank wall along one side
Checked map, another fluke: it's Tre-gynwr!
Could see train and bus stations. 'Fancy a beer'

Quickly changed and headed right on down
To have a relaxed sticky beak round town
At the bus station did some detailed scanning
Bus / train routes / times – even some planning!

Found a good pint but nowhere to eat
Back to CV to cook myself some meat
Reflected on a most enjoyable day
Chatting with many good folk on the way
I'd finished ahead of my cunning plan
And found a great place for parking the van

Woke to the sound of kids messing around
So dressed and breakfasted with scarce a sound
Drew back the curtains, hopped out the side door
As though most natural thing you ever saw
More kids at the bus stop across the road
Completely ignored me as passed them I strode
Thinking how great a parking place it was
Quiet yet central but also because
Only two hundred yards off the route I was going
So no time nor steps wasted toing and froing
As I walked down the hill I took in my stride
A mobile home – or a huge bike outside?

I Wish They'd Make Up Their Minds!

Have I mentioned at all there'd been plenty of rain?
Well now comes a part where it tested my brain
A muddy yard led to a sign for the path

I thought to myself 'You're having a laugh'
Pointed up the edge of the field on the right
Bottomless mud topped with stinking cow shite
About thirty cows slopped and slid up the track
Each secretly hoping I'd fall splat on my back
I followed them up and over the brow
Pleased that I wasn't a silly old cow
Down to a narrow bridge fording a stream
Just where the coast path led so it would seem

As a stile at this end stopped cows getting across
They slopped through the stream not giving a toss
Slipped and slid up the bank and onto a track
Where another sign pointed up and over the back
Some doubled back and were now at my rear
Cutting off my retreat? No, mustn't show fear
Started to cross but cows started to bellow
Have I mentioned before I'm no country fellow?
The cows and their calves were increasingly jittery
Cause and effect, the route ever more shittery

Concerned not to get between mother and calf
Thought I might give ground a mile and a half
Go back to the road and make my way round
A few extra miles but at least solid ground
I'd first have to wade through the horrific mud
Now even more covered in disgusting crud
Decided against, not sure why but I'd say
I felt I should find a more positive way
So stood for ten minutes hoping to find
Cows had the solution – 'Now make up your minds
I have to get going, I can't wait here all day'
But it seemed the cows could. Then I heard Parki say

"You're really pathetic expecting this herd
To find the solution – it's really absurd
In the pub this evening you'll tuck into a steak
Pull yourself together and ACT for muck's sake.
The cows can't get out at the top without harm
You're blocking their only way back to the farm
You're the one with the brains – or so you would claim
But your failure to work it out's really quite lame.
Key point in the problem is really quite clear
The cows will not move as long as you're here"

Harsh but fair. Went back to the start of the bridge
Forded the stream then climbed up on the ridge
Twenty feet up among bushes and trees
Clearing the path for the cows 'If you please
You've had plenty of fun, now I must get on track
Your route is now clear so pray head on back'
And that's what they did, still slopping and slipping
Back to the farm, their hindquarters still dripping
I scrambled back down to where the cows had been
And sure enough there was a stile I hadn't seen
The cows had been trapped, not just being stroppy
Not much of a life, all slippy and sloppy

Entertainment

Two more stupidly muddy fields led me to a grin

For TOWIE is a TV soap my nephew Ricky's in
'The Only Way Is Essex' is what the word stands for
I guess it's meant for younger folk, I find it quite a chore
Full of enlarged busted girls with botox in their lips
An Essex girl's foreplay is "Will you hold my chips?"
Hairless boys with weird tattoos each just like the others
Showing off the same six packs – a merry band of brothers
Every episode the same, dancing in some club
Spending someone else's cash drinking in the pub
When I saw the above sign it made me laugh out loud
Imagining retired Ricky and pensioned TOWIE crowd
In slippers and cardigans, pipe smoking, drinking scotch
Moaning 'bout the youngsters and the TV crap they watch

Carmarthen station mid afternoon
Didn't want to get to van too soon
Stopped at a cafe for tea and toast
Chatted to a woman 'bout... walking the coast
Waiting for her daughter to finish college
Enquired of her entertainment knowledge
"Try the pictures, you'll find Skyfall's on"
Pondered effect of mad cows on James Bond

Making Tracks

Next day I was back in deep brown sticky stuff
Very sorry for myself 'Enough is enough
The Wales Coast Path's not a good place to be
My luck will run out eventually
Sooner or later I'm sure to slip over
Be covered in cow crap rather than clover'

Out the field, down a track I met this guy
Said with a caring concerned look in his eye
"My name's Malcolm, Wales Path Engineer
Been trying to sort this stretch nearly all year
Doing my best but it rains every day
You're walking the path, tell me is it OK?"

I guess I was the best person to ask
Thought of his efforts and thankless task
Ceaselessly working in mud, endless rain
Like Sisyphus' stone again and again
'Yes, I am and its great, enjoyed every mile'
Beemed straight in his face and he started to smile
I grinned and he laughed, with a twinkling eye
"Except for the bits where mud's up to your thigh?"
Malcolm made gates, bridges and stiles
Maintaining the path for miles and miles
Made the waymarkers and erected them all
Using a very neat hole digging tool
Apologised for the mud (hardly his fault)
And lack of waymarkers but he'd been caught
It had been so wet for the past year they
Did emergency maintenance most every day
Started to reflect on Malcolm's daily grind
And appreciate the problems besetting his mind
As I approached Llanstefan I spied a white van
And found Malcolm having a break "While I can"

He suggested a particular cafe for lunch
So seeking a light snack I followed his hunch

T'was a café, post office and general store
As I ate my meal the rain started to pour
Heavier and heavier, persistenting down
I started to think I might actually drown
The cook and postmistress soon pointed out
St Clears was too far in this weather no doubt
"Be dark well before you make it, you see
So I recommend aim instead for Llanybri
Catch the bus back to Carmarthen from there
These are the times, best get going, take care"
That would still keep me some miles ahead
So dumped my plan and used her's instead

Now had more time to enjoy local sights
Like Llanstefan castle and other delights
Amazed at the number of castles around
Seeming to occupy all the best ground
Whenever I asked any Welsh people 'Why?'
They just gave me a quizzical look in reply
Back on the road and who should I see
But Martin again – is he following me?
Sponsored by some coast walk carers group?
Or is it a Groundhog Day deja vu loop?
Was he an angel sent to keep me on track?
Or common or garden homicidal maniac?

Rain belting down, Martin offered a lift
Llanybri to Carmarthen at the end of his shift
This was such good news that I didn't see
A beautiful spaniel was now following me
Despite my concern it might end up lost
A dog angel was keeping me safe at all cost
When we met in Llanbri Malcolm agreed
We should seek out the owner "This puppy's in need"
We drove to the farm close to where it had started

They said "Its next door's. You're so golden hearted
Its coat is soaked through, would have probably died"
"You must be its angel" Malcolm suddenly cried

Poetic Justice

Drove Carmarthen to Llanybri for the 7.40 bus

Then another to Laugharne without making a fuss
To start walking back to Llanybri at 9.00
Should get there in daylight, so everything fine

Laugharne's impressive castle ruins overlook the shore
Where intricately patterned paths wind a mile or more
Strong ties with Dylan Thomas whose poetic duty
Was describe what is plain: Laugharne's natural beauty

Absentmindedly strolling, when half over a stile
I noticed something that forced me to smile
No fence attached! Could have just walked round
Things like that make me laugh when others may frown

Strolled up the hill at Amroth to Mellieha B+B
Hoping for a special night of warmth and luxury
Fantastic from the outside but inside even better
Guest lounge with log fire – you didn't need a sweater
The whole place oozed quality with extras everywhere
Made it special, homely and you felt so welcome there
Given steaming coffee pot, home made bread and cake
Then Radox in the bathtub soothing every ache
Luxurious bed and pillows soon had me away
Then breakfast in the sunlounge setting up the day
Miles along flat sandy beach heading for Pendine
Famous for land speed records quoted in this sign

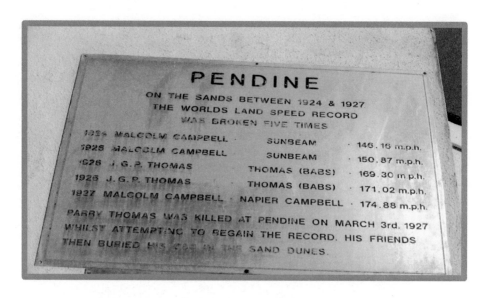

PENDINE

ON THE SANDS BETWEEN 1924 & 1927
THE WORLDS LAND SPEED RECORD
WAS BROKEN FIVE TIMES

1924	MALCOLM CAMPBELL	SUNBEAM	· 146.16 m.p.h.
1925	MALCOLM CAMPBELL	SUNBEAM	· 150.87 m.p.h.
1926	J.G.P. THOMAS	THOMAS (BABS)	· 169.30 m.p.h.
1926	J.G.P. THOMAS	THOMAS (BABS)	· 171.02 m.p.h.
1927	MALCOLM CAMPBELL · NAPIER CAMPBELL · 174.88 m.p.h.

PARRY THOMAS WAS KILLED AT PENDINE ON MARCH 3rd. 1927
WHILST ATTEMPTING TO REGAIN THE RECORD. HIS FRIENDS
THEN BURIED HIS CAR IN THE SAND DUNES.

Pendine Sands to Laugharne is what my map showed
But an army firing range forced me to use the road
Didn't want to be shot at by any form of rocket
Horse very pleased to see me – or gun in its pocket?

Laugharne views as stunning as they'd been the day before

No wonder Dylan Thomas spent his birthday on the shore

Is it me or are these vans heading for a fall?

Unlike Tenby with extensive well maintained town wall

Solid harbour, bright painted but strong every house
Classic lifeboat slipway – all feelings of safety rouse

A series of rocky coves leads on to Saundersfoot

To avoid cliff diving take care where your foot you put

Stacks and Packs

Stackpole's a fascinating place, wonderful to see
Incredible rock formations and how they came to be
Display boards depicting how 400 million years ago
Other side of the equator deposits were to grow
Crunched into each other like a rugby scrum
Twisted, bent and buckled, no-one to cry "mum"
Travelled four thousand miles to become part of Wales
Geological facts like these help balance your scales

arall y cyhydedd.

Sandstone
Look left – the red rocks
you can see were made from river
sediment 400 million years ago. Then, Wales was
part of a massive continent on the other side of
the equator.

Limesto
Look right
travel forw
and north
was under
made thes

Limestone

Look right and you travel forward 50 million years and north several hundred kilometres. This land was under water, and millions of tiny sea creatures made these limestone cliffs.

Crunch ti

Wales has tra
6000km in it
with a lot of r
them pretty cr

Crunch time

Wales has travelled nearly 6000km in its lifetime. Its rocks have had to put up with a lot of rough treatment, and it's left some of them pretty crumpled…

Turned to see the current world's tidal forces storm
Tearing at the surfaces, caves and arches form

Yet another brilliant day, said a silent 'thank you' there
To my nature-god who I believe cannot answer prayer
For to me it seems obvious a god who's just and fair
Cannot answer one soul's plea and leave another bare

The Best Laid Plans

Two nights booked at Herbrandston, Upper Neeston Lodges
Luckily the owners warned me of two local dodges
Tidal river crossings between Milford Haven and Dale
Then printed tide and bus tables to help me plan the trail
It took me several hours but I hatched a cunning plan
Feeling confident I could dodge fire and frying pan
Even catered with the dirth of buses on a Sunday
My hours of planning should ensure each one was a fun day:
Saturday park Milford Haven, from there walk to Dale
Timed to fit the tides for river crossings on the trail;
Sunday Milford Haven to Monkton, key stratagem:
National Express to Johnston! thence train to Haven M

Thinking 'Let's go OTT with my planning, so cunning'
Phoned to check the Dale to Milford H bus would be running
At first the woman flat denied they ran such buses ever
When she found the right timetable I just mumbled 'clever'
My checking was most fortunate as though it seems unsteady
The bus ran only by request from folks on board already!
So if I wasn't on the bus it wouldn't go to Dale
To be requested for the trip back: bad logical fail
'But people on the bus to Dale won't want to catch it back'
She talked as if I was the idiot, mine the mental lack
"You must request it in advance so the driver is aware
Otherwise he won't know so why would he go there?!"

Milton Haven is oil industry writ very large and clear
But I was soon far out of town 'much more attractive here'

River crossing's easy when the stones are high and dry

This planning has advantages – pleased I gave it a try

Dynasties

Henry Tudor landed here with four thousand men
Gathered more in Wales, set off East and then
Defeated Richard the Third at the Battle of Boswell
Setting himself up as The King, and his kids as well
Should I be more ambitious – make such a bid for glory?
Nah, I'd do a lousy job- and who would write this story?
Think I will just carry on walking round the coast
Maybe in some dark car park I might meet Richard's ghost

Anyway, gone are the days when you became King by force
I guess I could make an offer 'Your Kingdom for a horse?'

I'd arrived in time to walk the headland round from Dale
Useful as would later ease my further northward trail
Even after these extra miles back at the bus stop by four
Sat on a bench watching kids skim pebbles off the shore
Soon the sun set, it grew very cold, eveyone else had gone
I sat and shivered on the bench every stitch of clothing on
I'd checked the bus so knew it was arriving after five
So needed to keep myself warm if I wanted to survive
Realised I'd generate some heat if I moved around
So went for a walk! until at last I heard the welcome sound
Of a large vehicle approaching, then yes, the bus appeared
Was so relieved and thankful I let my feelings out and cheered
One passenger alighted, I was shocked when the driver said
"You're lucky I am dropping Meg. Should have booked ahead"

Pembroke Pipe Works

Every few miles around here I'd found myself encaged
No need to complain though, nor to get enraged
For when the path crossed pipelines or passed an oil depot
Cages stopped dodgy folks (like me) interfering with the flow

Used the A477 bridge to cross to Pembroke Dock

Crowded boats in the marina below proving quite a shock

The anchors in this statue almost seemed to be dancing

Perhaps the Pembroke Hornpipe? I found it quite entrancing

Bad Rhyme Time

My path followed the river to Pembroke's ruined castle

Could anyone resist the cry: 'get down you dirty rascal'?

Trust

Time to kill before my coach so no need to hurry
Window shopped for a bit then went for a curry
Luckily left 5 mins early because the coach did too
Luxury seats, dark and warm along the road she flew
I was scared I'd fall asleep or we'd get there late
But Johnston station bang on time, just 7 minutes' wait
Two bare platforms with no lights, signs or other peeps
Fearful of a mugging, such places give me the creeps
Beginning to have doubts when saw lights down the track
Thought 'Oh, ye of little faith' as I grabbed my sack
Felt a fool as I waved my hands to be sure it stopped
Suddenly back in warmth and light as on board I hopped
Loads of people sat and stared – I guess I was a sight
Apparition in their cosy world – but did I hear that right
"Welcome to new passengers hope you weren't too lonely
Remember for another time, Johnston's request stop only"

Day	Start	End
79	Baglan	Langland Bay
80	Langland Bay	Port Eynon
81	Rhossili	Llanmadoc
82	Llanmadoc	Loughor
83	Port Eynon	Rhossili
84	Kidwelli	Loughor
85	Carmarthen	Kidwelli
86	Carmarthen	Llanbri
87	Laugharne	Llanbri
88	Llanbri	Amroth
89	Manorbier	Amroth

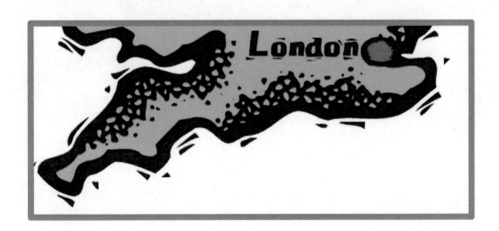

Next morning at the bunkhouses the woman wasn't there
I thought I'd paid her in advance but I couldn't swear
Man agreed to check with her then drop me a line
If it seemed I hadn't paid a cheque would be just fine

Drove CV to Broadhaven seeking a place to stay
Though I didn't have much faith tried the local YHA
Justified as it was closed except for pre-booked groups
Shrugged my shoulders, parked CV, tightened up my boots

The Ocean cafe / restaurant was serving morning coffee
Had a pot and bought a treat: bar of brazil nut toffee
A very stormy / windy day and boy the sea looked rough
Several times blown off my feet but I'm becoming tough

An onshore wind so I was safe even on exposed headland
Scene around exhilarating, dramatic, thrilling, grand
Foam ripped off the raging surf then flying through the air
Deposited on shore and cliff, white blanket everywhere

Skomer Marine Nature Reserve was open, dry and warm
Took my chance to spend an hour sheltered from the storm

Drank some coffee I had brought with me in my flask
I really think this planning lark is helpful in my task

Homing in on two Havens, Little (right) then Broad

Back to The Ocean where I said 'May I have a word?'
The waitress said "Use our car park, you'll be safe alright"
So collected CV from the YHA and set up for the night

Returned to Ocean's restaurant: home-made fish pie dinner
Hot and tasty so it seemed I'd really found a winner
Chatted to the owner who said "Sure, park here all week"
Turned in for a perfect night although the wind did shriek

Next morn eating cold cereal when I had the notion
'Scrumptious Captain's Breakfasts are served up in The Ocean
I've a cold, wet day ahead so need hot food inside
And can show off my Movember – latest source of pride'

No bus back so had to leave CV till Thursday night
Left her tucked up by a wall, sure she'll be alright
I'd rung a Solva B&B where they had two rooms free
Double en-suite 75 pounds or box room for just 30

Which one did I go for? Well, if I need to mention
You better go back to page 1, haven't paid attention
Foaming waves at Newgale Sands, Newgale near the cliff
Beach of painful pebbles, not sand, left me tired and stiff

Lunch traditional Welsh Cowl: lamb stew and cheese sandwich
Left CV's keys upon the bar, local put them in my hand which
Was a very thoughtful move – but another lousy rhyme
Will ensure both keys and rhyme chime next line and time

Barmaid took great delight telling me how hard and rough
Next four miles of coast would be: ups and downs and tough
As I clambered up the hill a scraping noise caused alarm
Like waves crashing on a pebble beach yet the sea was calm

Once above by looking back the culprit was revealed
A dredger digging drainage routes from saturated fields
It looked precariously poised on the end of the pebble bank
I half expected to witness as it first toppled then sank

I'd often fought my way along paths ruined by the rain
Mud deep in the middle, slippery edges causing strain
My tactic was one foot each side, slip sliding like a skier
Crazily singing my 'Shalooop-dop' song to the tune 'Maria'

Shaloop-dop

Shaloop-dop...
I just met some mud called shalooop-dop
And suddenly that sound
is coming from the ground again.
Shaloop-dop.
If it's light there'll be droplets spraying
If it's deep my boots will soon find their way in
Just don't let me fall in I'm praying
Schaloop-dop
The nightmare's the rain looks like staying
Shaloop-dop
My boots just can't help themselves saying
Shaloop-dop

In Selva my B+B was "Number 35. Felin Gog"
Owner took one look and said "Man, you need some grog"
When she saw from my T shirt I was walking for PD
Gave me cash, coffee, packed lunch and my room all free

Richard showed me to my room, upgraded to a twin
I was the only guest that night, no one else was in
"You've run of the house, cooker/washing machine/TV"
Chucked all my clothes in the machine, no false modesty

Watching TV first time for months really was a laugh
Drank gallons of tea and coffee, soaked in a deep hot bath
Thinking "It's only ten more days before my winter break
Yes I still enjoy the walk but how my heart does ache

For my home, family, friends, Christmas and New Year
Desperate for a few weeks off then drag myself back here"

Collected clothes from radiators I had dried them on
Free breakfast in Number 35 'Thanks again' I'm gone.

Perfect day as I strode along the harbour half a mile

Up onto cliffs where flat grassland soon returned my smile
Peaceful serene with ripple waves, distant seagulls cry
A gentle breeze fanned me beneath a fluffy-clouded sky.

St David's would be my night stop but how far could I get?
Next day's forecast strong wind, rain, freezing cold and wet
'Want to take advantage of the fine weather today
Sixteen miles about right, St David's via Whitesands Bay'

Walking above Porthlysgi Bay saw a stranded canoe
There was no-one on the beach so I speculated who
Would have left a canoe there, was somebody in trouble?

Decided to call the coastguard said 'Get here at the double'

"No need to panic, sir, it's a wreck but hard to reach.
Someday when there's little on we'll clear it from the beach"
'Now that's a great idea, I thought someone was drowning'
So, I *nearly* saved a life, despite the coastguard's clowning

Clearly there was little on at St Justinian's life boat station
In St David's I might offer a prayer for better communication

Had time to climb Carn Llidi to see my route for the morrow
When, given forecast weather, I'd be drowning in my sorrow

In St David's was pleased to find there would be evensong
Time to check into my B+B, freshen up then go along

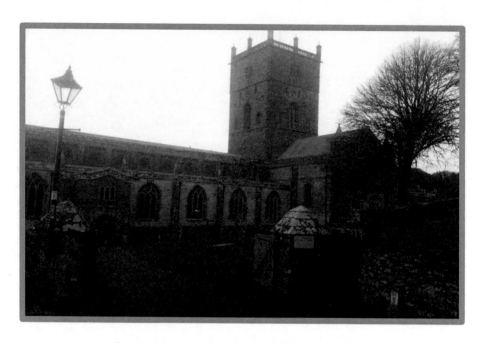

Expected a moving experience in this atmospheric site
The singing was truly excellent but the readings rather trite
Complete lack of enthusiasm, comment or explanation
A shame because, chosen well, each was about relations
With foreigners and adopted very different points of view
Love to have heard the Bishop's thoughts on the Old and New

Mr and Mrs B+B suggested an Indian in town
Splendid meal, excellent relations with foreigners all round
Forecasted gale with driving rain proved to be spot on
Condemned man had a hearty breakfast and then he put on
Two layers of thermals and waterproofs topped by hi vis jacket
Took a deep breath and set off, hoping somehow to hack it

Ten miles to Trefin, buses back to Broad Haven, his notion
Drive to Upper Neeston pay the bill drive back to The Ocean
For a hot meal, shower and well-earned peaceful night.
But as soon as I stepped outside I had an awful fright
It was so bad I couldn't risk the treacherous coast track
Particularly as the wind now blew straight into my back

Out on the coast it would be pushing me toward the edge
And I really didn't fancy a night stuck on some cliff ledge
If I was lucky – didn't care to think of falling to my death in
A tragedy, so plotted an inland road-based route to Trefin.
There were no other walkers and very few vehicles either
Several gave me funny looks (not the vehicle but the driver)
Seemed to delight in spraying me with muddy puddle water
Thinking if I was out in that I was getting what I oughter
Advert for sheepdog training made me feel none too clever
Sheepdogs have to 'do their thing' regardless of the weather
Wasn't prepared to risk the coast but tried another track
Footpaths crossing farmland could not be seen as slack

But it was just ridiculous cow-churned bottomless mud
And surely I had done my share of walking on such crud
One hundred yards in ten minutes, both boots waterlogged,
Gave up, returning to the road (hundred yards back slogged)
I had to be fair to myself – just what was I proving?
In howling gale driving rain and nothing much else moving

Yet I felt bad at 'giving in' to walking on the road
Nothing could get through those fields (perhaps a frog or toad)
Decided I had done my share, the cold and wet were numbing
Needed dry, heat and food which it seemed would be coming

This was a very welcome sign, I'd near thrown in the towel
Soon be chomping Welsh lamb chops or possibly Welsh Cowl

Cheered I pulled my hood up tight to shield the driving rain
Walked another quarter mile when this sign caused me pain

Trefin and pub now further than they were at t'other sign?!
I was soaked and freezing cold, couldn't wait to dine
But toyed with Abercastell just two more miles if the food
Dry out and warm up in Trefin's pub brightened my mood

Touched the coast at Aber Draw then up hill to the pub
Closed! And while I stood there bemoaning my lack of grub
A bus went zooming past toward St David's town: Oh dashit!
Then recalled there was a second route so I might still cash it
Checked my pocket timetable to find another shortly due
On the bus I slowly thawed as the puddle round me grew
At St David's had 15 minute's wait for the Broad Haven bus
My favourite driver Stacey drove it smoothly without fuss
Though some roads being flooded made her change her route
Said "Still walking in this weather you are a crazy coot"
Coffee and cake in The Ocean listening to locals state
How bad all the roads were and "You'd deserve your fate

288

If you ventured out upon them unless you really must"
Decided to post a cheque rather than in my luck to trust
Driving to Upper Neeston and back in the floods and dark.
Quiz night in The Ocean, joined John and Jan for a lark
We won – seventh prize in the raffle. Put CV's heater on
To warm and dry it, me, my clothes then put the lot on
PJ's, fleece, liner, two sleeping bags and double quilt
Cuddling HWB peacefully snored with no thought of guilt

It was fantastic to wake next day to a glorious morn
Even more so given the previous day's horrendous storm
As it was not Tues, Thurs or Sat I needed another plan
With no tourist buses running I would have to leave my van
At Trefin, then walk to spend the night near Strumble Head
Catch bus back to CV Saturday night – planning isn't dead!

I stepped up onto the grassy bank for a close up of this sign
Stepping down a bramble runner round my boot had twined
Cartoon moment as hands and boots scrambled to get back
In suspended animation – then crashed down on hard tarmac
Surely a broken back or rib? But as in many another slide
Rucksack took the main force so only damage to my pride

Meeting John Jones around four at the lighthouse's car park
Sun going down I started to think of being left in the dark
If he didn't show I'd have to walk to Goodwick say four miles
Nothing I couldn't cope with but it would add to my trials
Began to think of all the other people I had trusted
To be there when I needed, or my coast walk could be busted

Bus train drivers, shopkeepers, B+B and hotel owners
Everyone a helping hand to us wild adventure loners
Everyone a stranger yet my faith in them proved sure
Everyone my angel as I capered round the shore

My faith in John reflected as he showed his faith in me
"We are going out tonight, so once you've had your tea
Please relax in the living room, the telly may delight
We'll not be back till very late so wish you now good night"

Had breakfast and admired their mugs but then all too soon
John drove back to Strumble Head which really was a boon

To catch the bus through Fishguard back to Trefin and CV
I'd need to crack on 'cause it left Dinas at half past three

"Have you seen much wild life on land, the sea or shore?"
'Quite a bit but few seals, I'd like to have seen more'
"I think your luck's about to change, so no need to fuss"
On a beach near Carregwastad Point I saw a hundred plus

Marine Walk round the harbours of Goodwick and Fishguard
The French were there before me but had found invasion hard

From the old fort just four miles and I overlooked Pwllgaelod

Turned inland for Dinas where this old tractor stood

Chatted to a woman who'd been mucking out horse stables
Thinking 'Boy, she looks a mess' when she turned the tables
"Guess you must be sleeping rough, down upon your luck?
Here's a fiver, not for beer, buy yourself some tuck"

Had booked to stay at Tycanol, Newport Sands *next* night
Well passed by then so rang to ask 'Can I come tonight?'
The owner instantly agreed and said he'd give me lifts
So I could stay the next night too – I don't refuse such gifts
Solved the 'no bus' problem right round to Poppit Sands
Near Cardigan and from there I had a week of other plans!
Hil made me very welcome, joined him in the pub for dinner
Several pints, Thai green curry and I'm still getting thinner
A morning lift to Careg Aderyn "Much better walk that way
As its downhill from Cemaes Head to Newport, so they say"

And so it was, in glorious sun despite now late November
With views just like the one above so easy to remember
At Newport Sands a long detour to cross a minor river
But if I'd tried to swim across it would have made me shiver
And as reward for being good I saw this splendid sight
Two ladies splashing muddy puddles shrieking with delight

'Wait a minute. That's CV!' I was back at Tycanol farm
In time for lunch, a pleasant change which would do no harm
Make myself a brew and bite, relax for an hour or so
Admiring the view across the bay until 'It's time to go'

Confirmed Hil still OK to meet in the pub in Pwllgaelod
Then set off to beat him there as rain fell splish splash splod

Nice and relaxed, strolling along a muddy stretch of trench
I suddenly had an 'OMG' rather like Dawn French
When as the Vicar of Dibley she was taking a gentle stroll
Her body (my foot) sank into a bottomless mud-filled hole
Lucky for me my other foot found a very solid base
I stood back up unlike DF who disappeared without trace

All afternoon it rained hard which helped wash the mud off
Round Dinas Head in belting rain to the pub at Pwllgaelod
I was greeted like a hero as I charged through the door
Water pouring off my clothes and puddling on the floor
Sat by a roaring fire with a coffee, two pints and Welsh Cawl
Before Hil arrived and took me on a local's local pub crawl

Next night's lodging was with Jane Davidson in St Dogmaels
Decided to leave CV at Mwnt (hope you can follow my trails)
Walk to Careg Aderyn where Hil dropped me two days ago
Then back to Poppit Sands from where St Dogmaels buses go

Being a National Trust member, parking at Mwnt was free

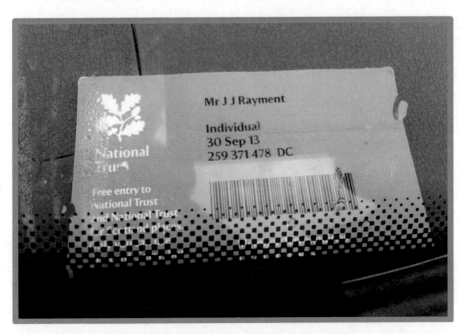

Took my card out of my wallet but the wind tugged it free
Where it went I knew not so took out another card
Threw it up into the air but this time watching hard
It shot off some 20 yards and showed no sign of slowing
Me feeling very stupid, fear of losing two cards growing
Gave chase, kept it in sight, caught and hung on hard
Ridiculously pleased I'd kept my losses to one card
Walking back toward CV eyes focused on the ground
Then after but a few paces my NT card I found
My daft idea had worked and now I felt very cheered
'But if I hadn't let go the first...' psychology is weird!

Having weathered this flying start the day followed my plans
Jane agreed to meet me at the café near Poppit Sands
She thought it better to move CV along the coast a jog
Drove me to Mwnt then led the way along to Llangrannog
While Jane cooked dinner in the best kitchen I've ever seen
I tried to make myself look smart – I think I managed clean
Jane said she'd been a member of the Welsh Assembly
Then decided to get a proper job and moved into HE
In the WA the Welsh Coast Path was under her umbrella
"Hope it hasn't been too wet" – I'd not the heart to tell her!

Next day Jane drove me back to Mwnt to safely hand me on
To my next minders, Ann and Richard Phillips, whose son

Had suggested my cause to them and lovely Ann had sent
A fantastic email – you may recall this is how it went:

"You don't know me but as you'll see
My son gave your address
My hubbie's a walker – I'm more of a talker
And as you may well guess
I'll cook you dinner, our bed's a winner

I think I can confess

Checked your dates and at this rate
Mwnt's November 26
If you care he'll meet you there
Details we can fix
Walk four days – he knows the ways
So you can just take pics

Then each night if it's alright
And doesn't mean a fuss
Dinner B&B without a fee
You can stay with us
I'll drive the car to where you are
Much better than the bus"

November the twenty-seventh and we three were there
Bang on time and target and showing few signs of wear

Immediate friendships blossomed as Richard led the way
I could just relax, enjoy, Ann and the dog could play
Richard cycles two thousand miles in summer to keep trim
"Walking's for the winter" – may struggle to keep with him
Knew all the paths and sights, told me stories as we went
Of local history, geography, characters, events
"Mwnt's famous conical hill with church built just behind
Hid from marauding Vikings: out of sight is out of mind

Chalets from railway carriages – and they're looking grand

Tresaith's a quiet, neat village leading uphill from the sand

Aberporth's in the background, see, just beyond that cliff"

Hang on just a minute – does he look a little stiff?!

When I said that to Richard, he laughed until he cried
"Well you look like Rudyard Kipling – a week after he died!"

At Llangrannog we enjoyed a cup of coffee in the van
Then I saw the value of Jane's "let's move it there" plan
Took an opportunity would have been rude to shelve
Went to spend a penny in 'Loo of the Year 2012'!

We arrived at R and A's house to be met by tea and cake
"While I cook the evening meal a shower you can take"
Richard washed and cleaned my boots while I had a nap
Then laid out a vast array of fillings, bars and wrap
So we could make packed lunches for the next day's walk
It was a walker's dream hotel, with laughter in their talk
Ann's delight to see Richard exhausted with blistered feet
Was so infectious even he laughed. It really was a treat
They had routines and traditions which they shared with me
Always make your own porridge, pour your own cup of tea
And if you left a half-drunk mug ten seconds unattended
T'was whipped off to the dishwasher- untidiness offended
'Strictly' every evening, knew better than the judges
But whatever faux pas I made they held me no grudges
Magical and I kept getting goosebumps hardly daring

To believe how lucky I had been, how generous and caring
Fun company they were, always lively pleasant banter
With friends like these my last few days will be at a canter.

Glenn Strachan 'Green Issues' mad joined us for a day
I'm into 'Global Fitness' so keen to hear what he would say

These last few days were proving to be a pure delight
Great company and leadership, weather cold and bright
Richard keen on early starts so we met at half past seven
Though the sky was barely light sun rise made it heaven
The sun cleared the horizon then into the sky it soared
Crunched on ice-filled puddles the rising sun soon thawed
In no time Aberystwyth was in view across the bay
Met Richard and Glenn's wives there to end a gorgeous day
Finished by 2.30! Very early but with our pre-dawn start
We'd still done 13 miles, could cross them off the chart
Glenn was interesting to chat to with cheerful friendly face
Bought lunch, gave cash for PD and had set a cracking pace
Then it was back to Richard and Ann's to bathe in luxury
Richard again cleaning my boots, Ann cooking my tea

Chatting with Richard he said "We could finish at Ynyslas
That would match our weekend plans" (but not mine, alas)
About 8 miles from Aberystwyth (we had finished there)
Whereas my unspoken intention was to finish at Ynis-hir
7 miles further on which would normally have been OK
But "Friday afternoon Ann and I are going away"
His lack of time for fifteen miles before leaving was plain
But given their help and hospitality no way I'd complain
Or go alone (was sure Richard would have been a willing cab
But keen to spend the time with him and not act like a crab)
So we put our heads together and soon found another way
We agreed on Tre'r Ddol which would mean a 10-mile day
Richard loved these houses leading uphill out of Borth

"Fantastic views along the 3-mile beach looking North

Past the Dovey river, Aberdovey then on to Tywyn
Ultimately as backdrop the famous peninsular called Llyn

We were only doing ten miles so Aberystwyth wasn't far

On arrival Richard said I'd earned the right to 'kick the bar'

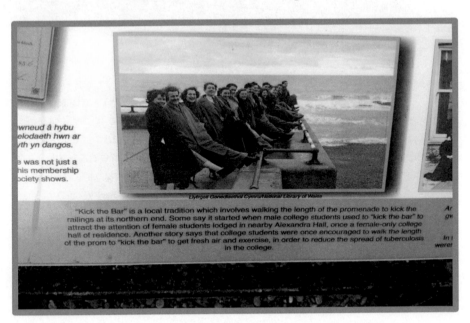

Llyfrgell Genedlaethol Cymru/National Library of Wales

"Kick the Bar" is a local tradition which involves walking the length of the promenade to kick the railings at its northern end. Some say it started when male college students used to "kick the bar" to attract the attention of female students lodged in nearby Alexandra Hall, once a female-only college hall of residence. Another story says that college students were once encouraged to walk the length of the prom to "kick the bar" to get fresh air and exercise, in order to reduce the spread of tuberculosis in the college.

And a celebration drink – 4 month's down just 8 to go
Crikey, where's my hair gone, I'll shiver in the snow

Ann drove to their house for a quick lunch and a shower
Then swift goodbyes and quickly off avoiding the rush hour
They'd said leave CV on the drive and suggested eateries
But very soon it was dark and cold and I started to freeze
Pub sign 200 yards away so thought I'd go and see
Roaring coal fire and varied menu. That will do nicely
Suddenly I noticed all the Christmas decorations
'Tomorrow its December, time I joined the celebrations'

You may be thinking, reader "He's taken it very well
Five miles short of target and not creating merry hell
Stopping now for three months – don't take me for a fool
There must be something missing, no way he'd be so cool"
Lynn's coming to Aberystwyth for a "TGI DONE" weekend
Arriving late afternoon next day: answer's there my friend
'Tomorrow up bright and early for just a few more miles
Then I can relax with no guilt pangs spoiling my smiles'
Pulled my chair close to the fire, gave my body a roasting
'Thanks again Richard and Ann' was my constant toasting

Drove CV to Tre'r Ddol and set off via Tre Taliesin
Was it Richard's leading or Ann's driving I was missing
Judging by these berries winter will be full of snow
Only thing I question is how do such bushes know?!

Be careful taking photos with sun low behind its said
Or may end up looking like the proverbial mushroom head

Machynlleth only 6 miles but not on coastal routes

Wouldn't do to cheat now, when I'm hanging up my boots
So its Dovey Junction but via the Wales Coast Path old thing
A great place to start from when I'm back again next Spring

Autumn sunlight sometimes seemed to sharpen every tree
While leaving other places rather dark and shadowy

'There's an art to photography even if taken on your phone'

"Then why don't you go and learn it and leave poetry alone?!"
Final stretch of path down to the road at Glandyfi
Hoped to catch the bus, then Winter Break for you and me

Soon found Dovey Junction, starting point in March '13

With great views across the Dovey to reflect on in between

Major roadworks and I feared the bus driver wouldn't stop
So I... walked on to find a place where on board I could hop
Vast network of scaffolding to help build a retaining wall

Another illustration of the hard work done to protect us all

Then bus and CV to meet Lynn and tell her all my tales
Spend a few day's quality time together in historic Wales

My spirits now were very high and I was satisfied
Happy with my decision making on which success relied
Detailed enough to avoid danger but loose enough to give
Variation and excitement which we all need to live
Physically walked 1762 miles and felt fitter than ever
Lost 22 pounds easily but while that may sound clever
People were saying "You look too thin, don't lose any more"
So I'll stuff the Christmas turkey – not too much of a chore

It seems that most adventurers who take a break midway
Never get back to the task, stuff just gets in their way
And though I'd walked for four months I had only done a third
I'd nearly quit a few weeks back - completion seemed absurd
So you and I must wait and see for though it's hard to equal
Achievements covered in this book - here's hoping there's a sequel

Day	Start	End
90	Amroth	Broad haven
91	Broad haven	West Angle
92	West Angle	Monkton
93	Milton Haven	Dale
94	Milton Haven	Monkton
95	Dale	Broad Haven
96	Broad Haven	Solva
97	Solva	St David's
98	St David's	Trefin
99	Trefin	Strumble head
100	Strumble head	Pwllgwaelod
101	Careg Aderyn	Pwllgwaelod
102	Mwnt	Careg Aderyn
103	Careg Aderyn	Cwmtydo
104	Cwmtydo	Llanon
105	Llanon	Aberystwyth
106	Aberystwyth	Tre'r Ddol
107	Tre'r Ddol	Dovey Junction